Kai's Power Tools

Filters and Effects

Heinz Schuller

New Riders Publishing, Indianapolis, Indiana

Kai's Power Tools

By Heinz Schuller

Published by:
New Riders Publishing
201 West 103rd Street
Indianapolis, IN 46290 USA

Printed in the United States of America 1 2 3 4 5 6 7 8 9 0

```
Schuller, Heinz.
   Kai's power tools filters and effects / Heinz Schuller.
   p.       cm.
   Includes index.
   ISBN 1-56205-480-5
   1.  Computer graphics.  2.  Kai's power tools.  I.  Title.
T385.S353 1995
006.6'869--dc20                                   95-33166
                                                      CIP
```

Warning and Disclaimer

Publisher	Don Fowley
Associate Publisher	Tim Huddleston
Marketing Manager	Ray Robinson
Acquisitions Manager	Jim LeValley
Managing Editor	Tad Ringo

Product Development Specialist
David Dwyer

Software Specialist
Steve Weiss

Senior Editor
Lisa Wilson

Development Editor
Linda LaFlamme

Technical Editor
Harry Magnan

Assistant Marketing Manager
Tamara Apple

Acquisitions Coordinator
Stacey Beheler

Publisher's Assistant
Karen Opal

Cover Designer
Karen Ruggles

Book Designer
Sandra Schroeder

Manufacturing Coordinator
Paul Gilchrist

Production Manager
Kelly Dobbs

Production Team Supervisor
Laurie Casey

Graphic Image Coordinator
Dennis C. Hager

Graphics Image Specialists
Becky Beheler
Jason Hand
Clint Lahnen

Production Analysts
Angela Bannan
Bobbi Satterfield
Mary Beth Wakefield

Production Team
Kim Cofer, Jennifer Eberhardt
Kevin Foltz, Aleata Howard,
Shawn MacDonald, Joe Millay
Erika Millen, Beth Rago
Gina Rexrode, Erich J. Richter
Christine Tyner, Karen Walsh,
Robert Wolf

Indexer
Bront Davis

About the Author

Heinz Schuller is a graphic designer based in Oak Park, Illinois. His one-man firm, Fly By Nite Studios, specializes in 2D and 3D graphics for multimedia and visualization applications. His clients include Mindscape (Navato, California) for which he created the animations for Complete Reference Library 3.0, a multimedia CD-ROM reference suite, and is designing the interface for the upcoming U.S. and World Atlas 6.0 products. Mr. Schuller teaches multimedia applications at Moraine Valley Community College in Palos Hills, Illinois, and performs architectural visualization services for Nederlander in Chicago. He recently designed the artwork for the Chicago band Voodoo Rain's new CD/cassette release entitled "Rusted" on Enormouse Records, and has written numerous review and how-to articles for Columbine's *3D Artist Magazine.*

Trademark Acknowledgments

All terms mentioned in this book that are known to be trademarks or service marks have been appropriately capitalized. New Riders Publishing cannot attest to the accuracy of this information. Use of a term in this book should not be regarded as affecting the validity of any trademark or service mark. Kai's Power Tools is a registered trademark of HSC Software, Inc.

Acknowledgments

This book would not have been possible without the incredible support I received from my wife Michele, who kept me inspired through the months of seclusion and was a saint about giving me the time I needed to write the book. We're hoping to become reacquainted now that I have a life again.

Thanks goes to the great staff at New Riders, including David Dwyer, Lisa Wilson, Stacey Beheler, Jim LeValley, and Steve Weiss, all of whom had extreme patience in working with me. Also thanks to Linda LaFlamme and Harry Magnan for their editing assistance.

Special thanks goes to HSC's Kai Krause, Daniel Prochazka, Phil, Scott, Kristin Keyes, Julie Sigwart, and the rest of the KPT team. Their assistance to me online while writing this book was invaluable, and I really appreciate the laid-back, personable attitudes posessed by the folks at HSC.

Also thanks to the following people who helped maintain a dialog on KPT in cyberspace, including Tim Cole for his help with application specific problems, Ernie Jackson, Heidi Waldmann, Barb McMillen, Adam Shiffman, Chris (The Faz), Mike Hell, Roger Moncrief, Stefan Claas, Laurie McCanna, and Bart (Biker26). The online community is rich with help as well as talent.

Lastly, I'd like to thank Rodney Fehsenfeld of Distant Design for allowing me to use some of his custom typefaces. Also thanks to Chris Schnieder for permission to use the Voodoo Rain artwork in my book. There's no place like H.O.M.E. Thanks to Ed Grskovich (the Mac Evangelist) for his Macintosh help.

Contents at a Glance

Table of Contents

Part IV Using KPT   171

Adobe CD Disclaimer

Licensor grants Licensee a non-exclusive sublicense to use the Adobe software ("Software") and the related written materials ("Documentation") provided by Adobe Systems Incorporated ("Adobe") to Licensor as set forth below. Licensee may install and use the Software on one computer.

The Software is owned by Adobe and its suppliers and its structure, organization, and code are the valuable trade secrets of Adobe and its suppliers. Licensee agrees not to modify, adapt, translate, reverse engineer decompile, disassemble, or otherwise attempt to discover the source code of the Software. Licensee agrees not to attempt to increase the functionality of the Software in any manner. Licensee agrees that any permitted copies of the Software shall contain the same copyright and other proprietary notices which appear on and in the Software.

Except as stated above, this Agreement does not grant Licensee any right (whether by license, ownership, or otherwise) in or to intellectual property with respect to the Software.

Licensee will not export or re-export the Software Programs without the appropriate United States or foreign government licenses.

Trademarks, if used by Licensee, shall be used in accordance with accepted trademark practice, including identification of the trademark's owner's name. Trademarks can only be used to identify printed output produced by the Software. The use of any trademark as herein authorized does not give Licensee rights of ownership in that trademark.

Licensee acknowledges that the Software is a "try-out" version of an Adobe product, containing limited functionality. Adobe is licensing the Software on an "as-is" basis, and Adobe and its suppliers make no warranties, express or implied, including, without limitation, as to non-infringement of third-party rights, merchantability, or fitness for any particular purpose. In no event will Adobe or its suppliers be liable to Licensee for any consequential, incidental, or special damages, including any lost profits or lost savings, even if representatives of such parties have been advised of the possibility of such damages, or for any claim by any third party.

If a shrinkwrap Licensee is used [Some states or jurisdictions do not allow the exclusion or limitation of incidental, consequential or special damages, so the above limitation or exclusion may not apply to Licensee]. Also some states or jurisdictions do not allow the exclusion of implied warranties or limitations on how long an implied warranty may last, so the above limitation may not apply to Licensee. To the extent permissible, any implied warranties are limited to ninety (90) days. This warrant gives Licensee specific legal rights. Licensee may have other rights which vary from state to state or jurisdiction to jurisdiction.]

Notice to Government End Users: If this product is acquired under the terms of a: *GSA contract*: Use, reproduction, or disclosure is subject to the restrictions set forth in the applicable ADP Schedule contract. *DoD contract*: Use, duplication or disclosure by the Government is subject to restrictions as set forth in subparagraph (c) (1) (ii) of 252.227-7013. *Civilian agency contract*: Use, reproduction, or disclosure is subject to 52.227-19 (a) through (d) and restrictions set forth in the accompanying end user agreement. Unpublished-rights reserved under the copyright laws of the United States.

Licensee is hereby notified that Adobe Systems Incorporated, a California corporation located at 1585 Charleston Road, Mountain View, California 943039-7900 ("Adobe"), is a third-party beneficiary to this Agreement to the extent that this Agreement contains provisions which relate to Licensee's use of the Software, the Documentation and the trademarks licensed hereby. Such provisions are made expressly for the benefit of Adobe and are enforceable by Adobe in addition to the Licensor.

Adobe is a trademark of Adobe Systems Incorporated, which may be registered in certain jurisdictions.

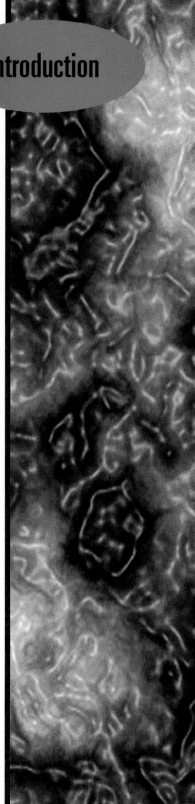

Introduction

Every so often a piece of software comes along that stands alone in its capabilities and potential. Software that stirs up a feeling inside you, like the one you had as a child when you got your first bicycle and thought, "Now I can really go places and discover new things." Software that, when you've read all the marketing hype, finally gotten the thing installed in your computer, and started it with huge expectations, exceeds those expectations and blows your mind. This is how I felt when I bought Kai's Power Tools.

I first became fascinated with procedural textures years ago when I stumbled across a free software program called Fractint, a fractal generator created by the Stone Soup Group. I had discovered the world of online communication and downloaded some pictures that had me baffled. "How can anyone paint this stuff?" I wondered as I gazed at the stunning, complex images. Slowly my new online friends sparked what has since become a life-consuming obsession and career.

My interest in fractals soon led to raytracing, a form of 3D rendering that simulates real-world physical properties like shadows, reflections, and refractions. At the time, graphical user interfaces for 3D programs were not available except on very expensive workstations. Instead, most people created pictures by typing elaborate descriptions into a text file, then feeding the file to a rendering engine to render the final image. In this text file, one would proceed to type a complete description of all the scene geometry, as well as the textures used on the objects and in the rest of the scene. No bitmaps were used as textures, so for many people significant time was spent tweaking procedural texture code to simulate textures like wood, metal, and glass. While I initially became interested in simulating real textures, I quickly became aware that I could create any sort of texture just by altering the parameters of the code. All of a sudden a brand new world of never-seen-before textures had opened up to me.

Naturally, designing textures in a text file is probably the least intuitive way to go about it. Visual feedback is non-existent, except when the image is actually rendered. This method of texture designing also made it difficult to achieve consistent, reproducible results. Furthermore, the process of learning the code and actually creating something decent looking took months of practice and trials with a lot of errors.

When Kai's Power Tools appeared, I immediately recognized it as being an insanely useful piece of software. Suddenly, all the complex underlying math was no longer an obstruction to getting at all the cool stuff. Having never been a serious graphics programmer, I was delighted at the prospect of exploring algorithmic patterns using a fun, powerful interface. Later, when KPT 2.0 was released,

I was amazed at the Realtime Preview that let me dial away like mad until I found something interesting. Here was a tool I could use for virtually any imaging application, from 2D to 3D and more.

Today KPT is an integral part of my work, and I couldn't live without it. In a commercial media-saturated world that constantly demands new and fresh graphical looks to fill its ever-expanding appetite for visuals, KPT has, in part, made it possible for me to compete and satisfy that appetite. Because a large part of my digital education has come from interaction with my online colleagues in cyberspace, I've made it a priority to give back knowledge by trying to help people in return. This book was written to help KPT users discover some of the joys of KPT that I've encountered, and I hope you find it useful.

New Riders Publishing

The staff of New Riders Publishing is committed to bringing you the very best in computer reference material. Each New Riders book is the result of months of work by authors and staff who research and refine the information contained within its covers.

As part of this commitment to you, the reader, New Riders invites your input. Please let us know if you enjoy this book, if you have trouble with the information and examples presented, or if you have a suggestion for the next edition.

Please note, though: New Riders staff cannot serve as a technical resource for Kai's Power Tools or for related questions about software- or hardware-related problems. Please refer to the documentation that accompanies Kai's Power Tools or to the applications' Help systems.

If you have a question or comment about any New Riders book, there are several ways to contact New Riders Publishing. We will respond to as many readers as we can. Your name, address, or phone number will never become part of a mailing list or be used for any purpose other than to help us continue to bring you the best books possible. You can write us at the following address:

New Riders Publishing
Attn: Associate Publisher
201 W. 103rd Street
Indianapolis, IN 46290

If you prefer, you can fax New Riders Publishing at (317) 581-4670.

You can send electronic mail to New Riders at the following Internet address:

ddwyer@newriders.mcp.com

NRP is an imprint of Macmillan Computer Publishing. To obtain a catalog or information, or to purchase any Macmillan Computer Publishing book, call (800) 428-5331.

Thank you for selecting *Kai's Power Tools Filters and Effects*!

Part *I*

What is KPT?

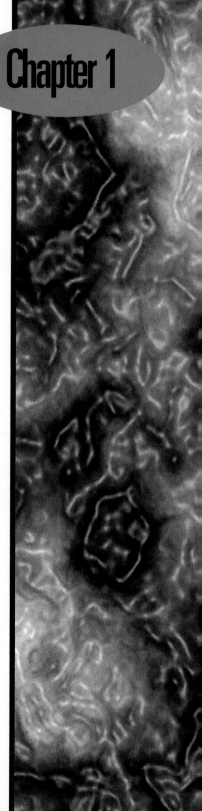

Chapter 1

Overview of KPT

kai's power tools

$\mathcal{K}$ai's Power Tools is a set of graphics tools for Macintosh and Windows-based computers. Unlike many software packages, Kai's Power Tools, otherwise known as KPT, was not designed to run as a stand-alone software package. Instead, KPT works in cooperation with other graphics programs, generating imagery and effects within them. These "other" graphics programs use a function, known as plug-ins, that enables you to "attach" third party programs such as KPT. The plug-in architecture present in these programs adheres to a plug-in specification created by Adobe Systems and implemented in Adobe Photoshop. KPT works with any program supporting the Adobe plug-in specification.

The types of effects that KPT creates are almost unlimited in scope. You can use KPT to create beautiful, complex gradients or color blends. You can create colorful texture fills or fractal patterns, or enhance your artwork with a dazzling array of filter effects. While some of KPT's effects are explosive, many are best used to subtly enhance an image or a portion of an image.

Third-party image-processing filters are not a new concept in the graphics world. An image-processing filter really is a piece of software code that performs a mathematical operation on a pixel or group of pixels within a digital image. The result of this mathematical operation is a change in the pixel's color characteristics such as hue, saturation, and intensity. Besides the standard filters present in most 2D graphics programs, packages such as Aldus Gallery Effects have been available prior to the release of KPT. These third-party filters usually work on existing images, and render effects such as glass distortion or painterly effects to the image. KPT includes over a dozen filters, providing a wide range of distortion, noise, and novelty effects.

What makes KPT unique is the inclusion of KPT's extensions. The extensions are a set of interactive graphics programs that include the Gradient Designer, Gradients on Paths, Texture Explorer, and Fractal Explorer. These extensions actually are fullblown programs that run inside the host plug-in compatible application (such as Photoshop). Each of the extensions enables you to create designs, patterns, and other graphical elements that overwrite or blend with the underlying image or selection.

The extensions are based on algorithms that generate graphics elements in three classes: gradients, textures, and fractals. By incorporating random functions, the extensions can generate an almost unlimited variety of these elements, from familiar-looking to never-before-seen. It is this wide variability that makes the extensions so interesting. In a world that continually demands new and fresh looks, the extensions are tools that help you escape from dull, traditional, or cliché designs.

With the KPT extensions and filters, you can begin exploring the world of algorithmic painting, where images start as one entity and mutate into countless possible variants.

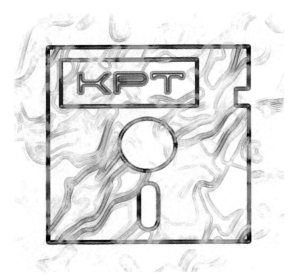

What Do I Need to Run KPT?

To run KPT you need a Macintosh or PC computer with a KPT plug-in compatible host application. The following section provides information on KPT's hardware and software requirements.

Hardware

The type of hardware you need to run KPT begins with the platform. KPT runs on the Macintosh and Windows-PC platforms.

On the Macintosh platform, you need one of the following systems:

◆ Macintosh II

◆ Powerbook

◆ LC

◆ Performa

◆ Centris

◆ Quadra

◆ Power Macintosh

The system should be running System 6.0.5 or later, preferably System 7. The system should have at least 8 MB of RAM, and a 24-bit graphics display is recommended (KPT will run on 8-bit displays in dithered mode). An FPU (floating point unit or math coprocessor) also is recommended and is required to run the Fractal Explorer.

For Windows, you need a 386DX-33 or better CPU, preferably with a math coprocessor (80387 for 386s, a 486 must be a DX class chip). The Fractal Explorer will not run without a math coprocessor. The system should be running Windows 3.1 in Enhanced Mode, and have at least 4 MB of RAM (and preferably 8 MB).

Graphics programs are among the most resource-hungry software you can buy. The optimal machine for running KPT is a Power Macintosh or Pentium-based computer, with enough RAM and hard drive space to meet your imaging requirements. Photoshop 3.0 needs at least 8 MB of RAM to run, and really needs 16 MB of RAM or more to run efficiently without swapping memory to your hard disk. Your RAM requirements might vary depending upon your application. Also, your output format might influence your machine requirements as well. People who work with large print images generally have machines with 64 MB to 256+ MB of RAM, with accelerated 24-bit displays. People who develop art for multimedia and small format applications can work comfortably in 32 MB of RAM or less.

Which platform (Mac or Windows) is better suited for your graphics needs? Historically, the Macintosh has been the leading platform for 2D imaging and photo retouching. In recent years, however, Intel-based personal computers running Windows 3.1 have become equally capable tools. Presently, the decision is more subjective than objective; pick whichever platform suits your needs best. KPT and Photoshop are nearly identical in the Mac and Windows implementations, and there is absolutely no difference in output quality or color. Arguing over which platform is best is similar to arguing over which hammer is better at driving in a nail.

Software

As previously mentioned, KPT works with any application that supports the Adobe plug-in specification. These are typically 2D paint and photo retouching programs, or in some cases video editing and animation programs. Programs that are known to be compatible with KPT include but are not limited to the following:

Installation and Files

Most of the previously mentioned software programs have a folder or directory designed to accommodate third party plug-ins. During installation, KPT prompts you for a destination for the KPT plug-ins and files. In most cases, you will specify the plug-in folder or directory specified by your plug-in compatible application. Once KPT is installed there, your plug-in compatible application should recognize KPT's existence the next time you run it, making KPT's tools available in your third party Filters menu.

If you use multiple applications that utilize third party plug-ins, you might need to install a copy of KPT for each application. If your application supports multiple plug-in folders or directories, you can install KPT in one area and specify this location in the host application's plug-in configuration. However, some programs (such as Photoshop/ Windows and Premiere/Windows) allocate their own exclusive directories, forcing you to install the plug-ins into each area separately.

KPT installs differently depending on the system you use. If you are using a Mac, KPT installs into the folder of your choice and creates a subfolder called KPT Support files 2.1. This folder contains the main filter hub (program) file, program help file, and the Preset hub files (factory and user Presets). Inside the support folder is another folder

Macintosh	Windows
Adobe Photoshop	Adobe Photoshop
Fractal Design Painter	Fractal Design Painter
Pixel Paint Pro 3	Aldus Photostyler
MicroFrontier Color It!	Fauve Matisse
Canvas	Corel PhotoPaint
Adobe Premiere	Adobe Premiere
Strata StudioPro	Altamira Composer
Avid Videoshop	Micrografx PicturePublisher
JAG II	Caligari trueSpace

called Cyclone ArbMaps that contains external ArbMap files for KPT's Color Cyclone filter. The total disk space required for the standard KPT files is around 2.7 MB. Optionally, you can install the KPT Extras, which creates a folder containing about 1.5 MB of sample images and utilities, bringing the total disk space required for complete KPT installation up to around 4.2 MB.

If you are using Windows, KPT 2.0 installs into the directory of your choice, where it puts all of the filter files (*.8BF) and Preset hubs (*.GRD, *.TEX, *.FRX). The main filter hub file and program help file are installed into the Windows directory. The total disk space required for the standard KPT files is around 5.5 MB. Optionally, you can install KPT Extras, which installs a sample image and "Kai's Power Tips" documents using an additional 5 MB, bringing the total disk space required for complete KPT installation to about 10.5 MB.

Mac KPT versus PC KPT

As of the writing of this book, the latest versions of KPT are 2.1 (Mac) and 2.0 (PC). The Macintosh and PC versions of KPT are virtually the same, but the Mac version of KPT includes four filters not available in the PC version. These filters are as follows:

◆ Gaussian Glow

◆ Gaussian Electrify

◆ Gaussian Weave

◆ Color Cyclone

The PC/Windows version of KPT has some features not found in the Macintosh version of KPT. Most notably, in the Windows KPT Texture Explorer there is a function known as the Equalizer. The Equalizer enables users to fine-tune the parameters of a texture created in the Texture Explorer extension. See Chapter 5, "The Texture Explorer," for more information on the Equalizer. Also, the PC/Windows version of KPT enables the

user to start the Gradient Designer Extension directly from the Texture Explorer or Fractal Explorer extensions, giving the user the ability to edit a texture or fractal's color properties within the given extension. This capability is not found in the Macintosh version of KPT.

The KPT user interface controls for the Mac and PC versions are almost identical in design as well as functionality. One difference between the platforms is a primary keyboard key used during many KPT operations. On the Macintosh, this is the ⌘ key. The equivalent on the PC is the Control key, or Ctrl. The Standard Cut/Paste commands are ⌘+C/⌘+V on the Macintosh, and Ctrl+C/Ctrl+V on the PC.

KPT Fundamentals and Concepts

Before using either KPT's extensions or filters you must start your plug-in compatible application, then open a new or existing image on which to operate. This image is known as the underlying image when working with KPT, and it will receive the effects of any KPT operations you perform. This underlying image must exist before you can perform any KPT functions.

KPT does not require you to operate on entire images at once. You can operate on "selections" or selected areas of an image, also known as paths or friskets. Selections are an arbitrarily bounded area defined by using some sort of Marquee, Lasso, or Path tool in your host application (see fig. 1.1).

Selections, once created, are displayed on-screen with a perimeter composed of moving dotted lines, known as marching ants. The marching ants define the boundaries of the selection (see fig. 1.2). In all cases, the selection path must be "closed," with no breaks or open areas around the perimeter. Selections can be rectangular, circular, or any other closed shape you can imagine.

A Selection typically defines a one-pixel wide border that separates the inside of a selection with the outside. This one-pixel border is represented by the marching ants line, and any operations you perform inside the selection will result in a one-pixel wide transition area between the inside and outside.

FIGURE 1.1

Photoshop selection tools.

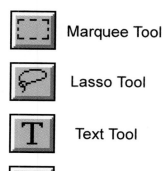

Marquee Tool

Lasso Tool

Text Tool

Magic Wand

FIGURE 1.2

Creating a selection.

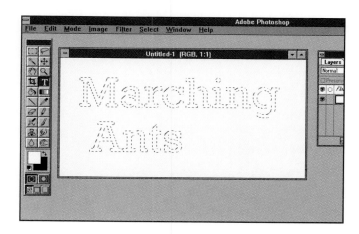

Selections also can be feathered, a function that increases the width of the transition area making the transition between the inside and outside of a selection smoother. Any effects filled or processed inside the selection will transition smoothly to the area outside the selection. The pixel width covered in this transition is known as the feathering width.

When you feather a selection, you have control over the feathering width (see fig. 1.3). This enables you to create sharp or smooth transitions between the inside and outside of selections. Because you can create any number of selections with different feathering widths in an image, the door is open for many interesting effects applied on selected areas. The KPT Gradients on Paths extension uses feathered selections as the foundation of its effects. Gradients on Paths applies a gradient band that follows the perimeter of the selection path, with its width determined by the feathering width of the selection.

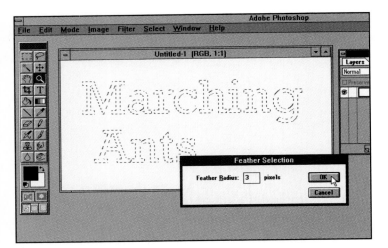

FIGURE 1.3

Feathering a selection.

When you have decided on whether to operate on the entire image or selected areas, you then can launch a KPT filter or extension. The filters operate in one step. Choosing a KPT filter from your host application's Filter menu will execute that filter's function and display the results on your underlying image.

The extensions operate a bit differently. When executed, the extensions display the KPT user interface. Depending on which extension you launch, the user interface might appear differently (see fig. 1.4).

Once launched, the extensions enable you to create a design and preview it in a window known as the Realtime Preview window. This handy feature enables you to preview your design before committing it to the underlying image. At any time, you can cancel the operation with no resulting effect on the underlying image.

Caveats for Non-Photoshop Users

KPT was designed to work primarily in conjunction with Adobe Photoshop, and much of the user manual terminology and concepts are Photoshop specific. Because many of Photoshop's features can be found in competing products, and because many of these products adhere to the Adobe plug-in specification, most KPT operations should work correctly.

Selections

The largest area of confusion for non-Photoshop users lies in the use of selections and feathered selections. Many of these non-Photoshop applications use different terminology when referring to these functions (see fig. 1.5). In Fractal Design Painter 2.0 and 2.1, for example, selections are known as friskets. In Fractal Design Painter 3.0 and 3.1, selections are known as paths. In addition, some applications refer to feathering as smoothing a selection.

FIGURE 1.4

The extensions user interface.

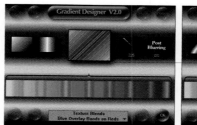

KPT Gradient Designer   KPT Gradients On Paths

KPT Texture Explorer   KPT Fractal Explorer

FIGURE 1.5

*Selections/feathering in Photoshop 3
and Painter 3.1.*

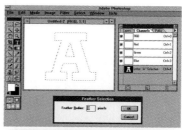

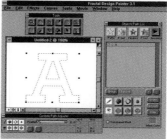

Alpha Channels

Another area of confusion for non-Photoshop users is the Alpha Channel (see fig. 1.6). A typical RGB image contains three channels: Red, Green, and Blue. Each of these channels contains 256 possible shades of their respective colors. When combined, the channels create an RGB image composed of up to 16.7 million possible colors (256×256×256).

Alpha Channels are one or more additional channels in an image that contain 256 possible shades of gray (from pure black to pure white). The Alpha Channel works in conjunction with Selections, and provides transparency or opacity information for the image. The Alpha Channel typically is used to specify which parts of an image contain transparency during a compositing operation.

In Photoshop, you can save any selection as an Alpha Channel, enabling you to reload the selection at any time. When the selection is reloaded, Photoshop looks at the Alpha Channel and uses it as a reference for building the selection. Wherever the Alpha Channel contains white, a selection area exists. Loading an all-black Alpha Channel indicates that there are no selections available. An all-white Alpha Channel indicates that the entire image is selected. Any shades of gray between pure black and pure white are interpreted as transparent selection areas, where the level of white relates to the level of transparency.

NOTE *Depending on which non-Photoshop application you are using, you might or might not have Alpha Channel capability. Look through your user manual for any references on Alpha, Transparency, Opacity, or Channel Operations to find out whether your non-Photoshop application supports the use of Alpha Channels.* ●

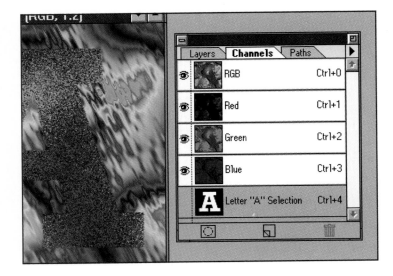

FIGURE 1.6

The Alpha Channel.

Technical Notes

If you are using a Mac and you experience system hangs or strange behavior while running KPT, they can usually be traced to incompatible INITs. Your mission is to figure out which INIT is causing problems and remove or modify it. This can be done under System 7 by starting your system with the Shift key depressed, which will turn off system extensions. Then, add the INITs back into the system folder one at a time until you run across the trouble INIT. Under System 6, you will need to remove all INITs from the system folder. If KPT runs correctly once the INITs have been stripped, then one or more of your INITs is the problem. Also, running AutoDoubler or another disk-compression program can cause problems if you compress the KPT files. Make sure that the KPT files are uncompressed on your hard drive.

If you are using Windows, it presents many interesting challenges for the programmer when it comes to memory management. Because of some inherent restrictions in the Windows operating system, two of KPT's filters (Glass Lens and Page Curl) will not operate on files that are 16 MB or larger. This limitation can be subverted by splitting your large image by channels into separate images, then applying the filters and recombining the channels. Also, please note that some of KPT's Extensions consume an inordinate amount of system resources. This situation can cause problems when running multiple applications along with KPT, generating low resource errors when you exceed the resource limits. The Texture Explorer in particular uses almost 40 percent of your total system resources (GDI and user). This situation has not improved with the release of Photoshop 3.0, which utilizes up to an additional 30 percent of system resources. To avoid problems, shut down all nonessential applications while running KPT to free up the maximum amount of system resources.

STOP *Be aware that there are limitations to running KPT 2.0 under some of the newer Microsoft operating systems, most notably Windows 95 and Windows NT. Because KPT is a 16-bit application, it requires a 16-bit host application to function, or a host that can run 16-bit plug-ins in 32-bit emulated mode. For this reason, KPT does not work with Photoshop 3.0 (a 32-bit app) running under Windows 95 or Windows NT. If you are using one of these operating systems, you will need to load a 16-bit application like Photoshop 2.5 to run KPT.*

KPT will run under 16-bit operating systems like Windows 3.1, Windows 3.11, or Windows for Workgroups. In these operating systems, Photoshop 3.0 (a 32-bit app) runs under the Win 32 extensions, emulating 32-bit sessions in a 16-bit operating system. At the time of the writing of this book, a 32-bit native version of KPT is under development. ●

Getting Started

The following chapters provide information about KPT's extensions and filters. It is highly recommended that you work through the extensions first because they provide the foundation for many of KPT's effects and operations. At a minimum, try to gain an understanding of the Gradient Designer extension because it is really the core module of KPT. Your time invested in learning the Gradient Designer's features is well spent, and should lead to many rewarding results. Now, roll up your sleeves and start having fun with KPT!

Part **II**

The Extensions

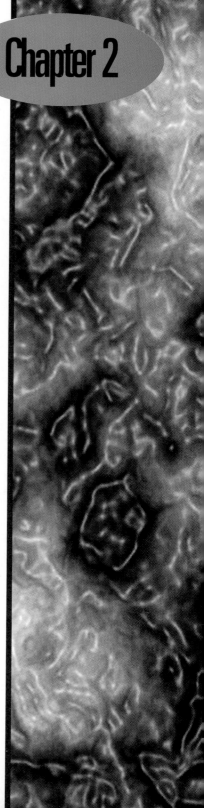

Chapter 2

Unraveling the Interface

$\mathscr{T}$he user interface is what you see when you start Kai's Power Tools Gradient Designer, Gradients on Paths, Texture Explorer, or Fractal Explorer extensions. The user interface gives you access to buttons, sliders, and other controls used to manipulate the graphics. Several components of this interface are common in all of the KPT extensions and are discussed in this chapter.

Interface Philosophy According to Krause

The KPT extensions user interface was designed by Kai Krause at HSC (the manufacturer of KPT). Krause's philosophy on user interfaces is the driving force behind many of HSC's products, and relies on the principle that the interface should "fade into the background and be forgotten and taken for granted." Subsequently, Krause made a complete departure from the standard user interface (UI) concept, abandoning traditional button labels, pull-down menus, and other common interface elements.

This novel approach essentially divides prospective users into two camps: those who love it and those who don't. Some users believe interfaces should be extremely easy to learn, incorporating copious labels, pass-over button help, and other popular help tools all simultaneously accessible on one screen. In contrast, others believe that interfaces will never evolve to higher levels as long as they must appeal to the lowest common denominator. Krause wants his users to explore the possibilities instead of being told how to use the program. "I'm not going to actually put in all these literal explanations because that ignores the process of exploration to find out what it is in the first place." What you see in the interface is what you need at the present moment, not every conceivable control thrown into one screen.

Regardless of interface philosophy, the KPT interface is well suited for the creation of algorithmic images. Its artful and interesting design stimulates and encourages exploration, leading to some truly satisfying and unique results. If you let go of some of the preconceived notions about how a program should work, you might find yourself liking it quite a bit.

Common Interface Elements

The KPT extensions actually are full-blown applications that run inside the host plug-in compatible application. You will use the extensions to design completely new graphics to fill or blend in with an existing image. The KPT extensions include the Gradient Designer, Gradients on Paths, Texture Explorer, and Fractal Explorer. The KPT user interface for these extensions has many components, each with a specific function. The components in the following section are common to each of the KPT extensions. Some of the options might be slightly different depending on which extension you are using, but their function essentially is the same.

Figure 2.1 displays the interface for the KPT Gradient Designer extension. Along the top of the window are the five main interface controls.

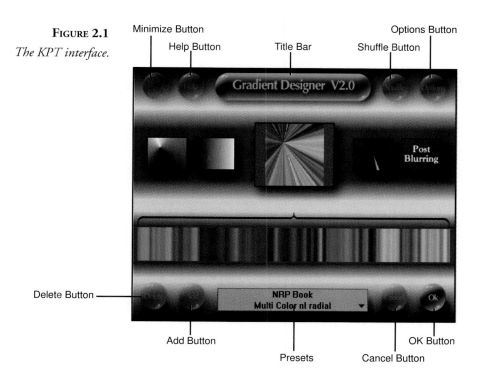

FIGURE 2.1

The KPT interface.

Minimize Button

Help Button   Title Bar   Shuffle Button   Options Button

Delete Button

Add Button   Presets   Cancel Button   OK Button

◆ **KAI LOGO/MINIMIZE BUTTON.** If you pass the mouse button over this button, it displays the program credits. This button has different functionality if you are using Mac instead of Windows. On the Mac, if you click on the Kai Logo the user interface is reduced to a minimal size, enabling you to see more of the underlying image. Click on it again to restore the user interface to full size. In Windows, double-click on the Kai Logo to shrink the interface to a smaller version. The Windows Gradient Designer alternately lets you Shift+double-click on the Kai Logo to shrink to just the three part Gradient Bar. In the Windows Texture Explorer and

Fractal Explorer, the minimization function produces a small moveable version of the Realtime Preview window. Double-click on any non-button area of the interface to restore it to its normal size.

◆ **HELP.** Clicking on this button brings up program help in a traditional help format. In Windows, context-sensitive help is available by pressing F1, which changes the cursor into a cursor with a question mark attached. In context-sensitive Help mode you can click on any part of the interface and receive help on the related function or topic. You can exit this mode by pressing Esc.

◆ **TITLE BAR.** The Title Bar displays the name of the extension in use. Clicking and dragging on the Title Bar lets you move the window and reposition it on the screen. The position of the window is retained in memory until you exit the KPT-compatible program you are using.

◆ **SHUFFLE BUTTON.** Clicking on this button produces a menu that enables you to randomly shuffle the major parameters in the current extension (see fig. 2.2). Shuffling enables you to create new designs from existing ones by generating random settings for the various parameters. By selecting the various options and toggling them on and off, you can control which parameters get shuffled. This enables you to test your current gradient design against one or more test images, or with other parameters.

◆ **OPTIONS.** This button displays a menu of options that includes KPT's Apply modes, preview options, and user preferences (see fig. 2.3). The following section examines each of these three groups under the Options menu in greater detail.

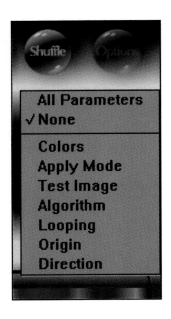

FIGURE 2.2
The Shuffle menu.

FIGURE 2.3

The Options menu.

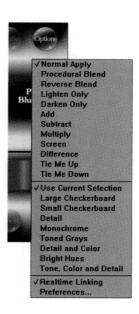

The Apply Modes: A Crucial Part of KPT

The apply modes are a crucial and powerful part of KPT, and control how KPT designs are applied to the current image. Whenever you design a gradient, texture, or fractal image using the KPT extensions and click on OK, KPT looks at the current image and decides how to apply the new KPT design to it. The Apply modes use mathematical algorithms to calculate how the new effect is applied to the original image. These algorithms are based on the Image>Calculate modes found in Photoshop.

The apply modes range from Normal Apply (a direct application) to blending apply modes like Procedural Blend, Reverse Blend, Lighten and Darken, Add and Subtract, Multiply and Screen, and Difference (see fig. 2.4). Windows users have two additional apply modes, Tie Me Up and Tie Me Down. The following section addresses each of these apply modes in greater detail.

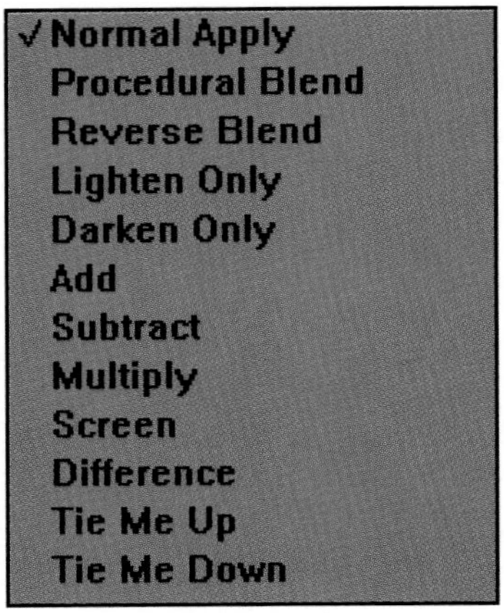

```
✓ Normal Apply
  Procedural Blend
  Reverse Blend
  Lighten Only
  Darken Only
  Add
  Subtract
  Multiply
  Screen
  Difference
  Tie Me Up
  Tie Me Down
```

FIGURE 2.4
The apply modes.

As of version 3.0, Photoshop's new Layers feature alternately gives you the option of separating your designs into layers. This enables you to arrange KPT designs into different layers, retaining control over how the layers interact. Using KPT in layers gives you complete flexibility and the ability to store several variations of an image in one file. Unfortunately, KPT extensions will not render to an empty (transparent) layer. This forces you to first fill the layer or selection with color, or utilize a Layer Mask, before applying a KPT filter. See your Photoshop manual for more information on Layer Masks.

The effects of the apply modes can be demonstrated using four sample images: a color spectrum, a color photograph, a grayscale ramp, and a grayscale rendered image (see fig. 2.5). While the effects that can be generated with KPT virtually are unlimited, these sample images, when shown next to the altered versions, can give you a reference point for your own operations.

Normal Apply

Normal Apply essentially takes what the user sees in the preview window and applies it to the current image or selection. In figure 2.6, notice how the gradient is applied to the three sample images. In each case, the sample image is totally overwritten by the gradient design created in the Gradient Designer. To enable Normal Apply mode, select it from the Options menu.

NOTE *If the gradient design includes transparency elements, the underlying image will show through.* ◆

In figure 2.7, the transparent sections of the gradient enable the underlying image to show through. The Gradient Designer has applied the transparent parts of the current gradient to the underlying image of color bars. Any gradient that contains transparent attributes will blend with the underlying image. Gradient transparency is applied similarly in all the apply modes.

FIGURE 2.5

Test images for apply modes.

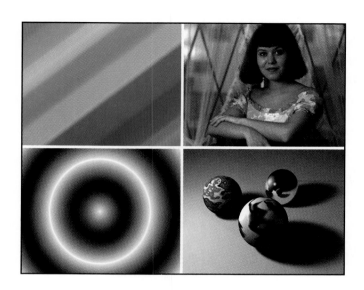

FIGURE 2.6

The Normal Apply mode.

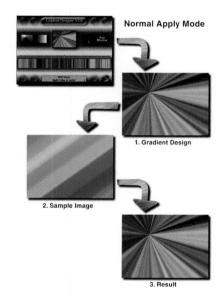

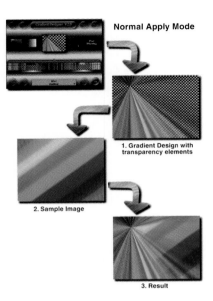

Normal Apply Mode

1. Gradient Design with transparency elements

2. Sample Image

3. Result

FIGURE 2.7
Normal Apply with transparency.

Procedural Blend

In figure 2.8, the gradient design is blended into the sample images. In each case, you can observe how the design adapts to blend with the current image.

The Procedural Blend Apply mode blends what the user sees in the preview window to the underlying image or selection using a procedural algorithm. The Procedural Blend operates by comparing the luminance values between the underlying image pixel and the new incoming pixel (processed by the KPT filter). If the underlying image pixel's luminance value is brighter than 128 (on a scale of 0-255), the new (KPT) pixel's value is adjusted by a similar amount before being added to the underlying pixel. If the underlying image pixel's luminance value is darker than 128, the new pixel's luminance is adjusted proportionally lower. This results in a more natural blend that follows the color contours of the original image. Areas that are completely black or completely white remain unaffected.

Reverse Blend

The Reverse Blend is similar to the Procedural Blend, but the underlying image pixel values are adjusted based on the values of the new (KPT-processed) pixel (see fig. 2.9). This is the opposite of what happens in a standard procedural blend. The new KPT pixels aren't adjusted and as a result, the subsequent image is weighted more heavily toward the new design instead of the original.

FIGURE 2.8

Procedural Blend Apply mode.

FIGURE 2.9

Reverse Blend Apply mode.

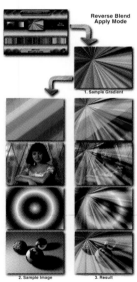

Lighten and Darken Only

The Lighten Apply mode compares the underlying image pixel with the new KPT pixel and computes which new KPT pixel has a lighter intensity than the underlying image pixel in each channel (see fig. 2.10). In an RGB image, for example, the lighten apply algorithm looks at the red, green, and blue channels. Wherever the intensity value of the new KPT pixel is lighter than the corresponding underlying pixel, the new KPT pixel is added. The resulting image generally will be lighter than the original.

The Darken Apply mode works opposite of Lighten Apply, adding new pixels only where the new pixel intensity is darker than the original pixel value. The resulting image generally is darker than the original (see fig. 2.11).

Add and Subtract

The Add Apply mode multiplies the intensity values of the underlying image pixel and new KPT pixel. Any pixel value equal to or exceeding pure white (255) is clipped at that value at white. The resulting image is generally lighter (see fig. 2.12).

The Subtract Apply mode subtracts the new KPT pixel color values from the underlying image pixel. In an RGB image, a mathematical operation occurs using the formula Red-Red, Green-Green, Blue-Blue, referring to the pixel color values. The resulting image reflects the differences that result from the formula, usually appearing darker than the original image (see fig. 2.13).

Figure 2.10
Lighten Apply mode.

FIGURE 2.11

Darken Apply mode.

FIGURE 2.12

Add Apply mode.

FIGURE 2.13

Subtract Apply mode.

Multiply and Screen

The Multiply Apply mode analyzes the dark components of the new KPT effect and applies only those dark components to the underlying image. The Multiply Apply mode operates on a linear scale from light to dark. The darker the pixel color value in the new KPT effect, the more the new KPT pixel will be applied to the underlying image pixel. Pure white pixels in the new KPT effect are ignored, and pure black pixels are applied to the underlying image at 100 percent. The resulting image is usually darker than the original (see fig. 2.14).

The Screen Apply mode works opposite of Multiply Apply mode. The lighter the pixel color value in the new KPT effect, the more the new KPT pixel is applied to the underlying image pixel. Pure black pixels in the new KPT effect are ignored, and pure white pixels are applied to the underlying image at 100 percent. The resulting image is usually lighter than the original (see fig. 2.15).

Difference

The Difference Apply mode is unquestionably one of the most interesting and wild-looking apply algorithms. The Difference Apply mode analyzes color values in both the new and original pixels. If the underlying image pixel is darker than the new KPT pixel, it is subtracted from the new KPT pixel yielding the difference. If the new KPT pixel is darker, it is subtracted from the underlying image pixel. The results of the Difference Apply mode can produce surprisingly beautiful results depending on the source images used (see fig. 2.16).

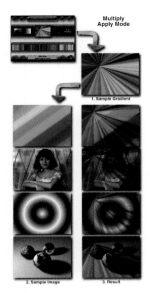

FIGURE 2.14

Multiply Apply mode.

FIGURE 2.15

Screen Apply mode.

FIGURE 2.16

Difference Apply mode.

Tie Me Up and Tie Me Down

Users of the KPT Windows version have two additional apply modes. The Tie Me Up and Tie Me Down Apply modes use algorithms similar to the Add and Subtract Apply modes, but instead of clipping the color beyond the black-and-white thresholds, they retain the clipped values as color values. Like the Difference Apply mode, they are somewhat unpredictable but can produce some very interesting results. The resulting images have interesting, aliased patterns with intense neon-like color variations (see figures 2.17 and 2.18).

FIGURE 2.17
Tie Me Up Apply mode.

FIGURE 2.18
Tie Me Down Apply mode.

The Realtime Preview Window

Near the center of each KPT extension window is a box known as the Realtime Preview window. This box enables you to preview your designs before you commit to applying them to your image. Each time you modify a parameter the window is updated instantly, hence the term "realtime." This feature can be turned off for users possessing slower systems. When turned off, the window waits for a "mouse-up" or non-depressed state before updating.

You can control what appears as a background in the Realtime Preview window by selecting one of the choices in the second group of the Options menu. Whenever your design interacts directly with an underlying image, either through transparency or using a non-normal apply mode, the background image provides a means of previewing the effects on a range of sample test images. These Preview options are as follows (see fig. 2.19):

◆ **USE CURRENT IMAGE.** Uses the current underlying image.

◆ **SMALL CHECKERBOARD.** Uses a small checkerboard pattern.

◆ **LARGE CHECKERBOARD.** Uses a large checkerboard pattern.

◆ **DETAIL.** Uses a detailed close-up of an eye.

◆ **MONOCHROME.** Uses a monochrome image of a U.S. relief map.

◆ **TONED GRAYS.** Uses a gray background with a colored globe.

◆ **DETAIL AND COLOR.** Uses a color photo of Kai and family.

◆ **BRIGHT HUES.** Uses a twirled bright color spectrum.

◆ **TONE, COLOR, AND DETAIL.** Uses a detailed Bryce landscape.

While the majority of your previewing might occur using the underlying image as a background, the eight sample backgrounds provide an excellent range of test images for previewing designs. Many times, it's worth scrolling through the test backgrounds to make sure you haven't missed any surprising color interactions.

The Realtime Preview window also becomes an extension-specific tool for manipulating your designs. Depending on which extension is in use, you might find yourself clicking in the Realtime Preview window to position, zoom, or blend your design with the underlying image. See the chapters on the Gradient Designer, Gradients on Paths, Texture Explorer, or Fractal Explorer for more details.

The Presets

The Preset window is located near the bottom of each extension user interface centered between two sets of round buttons (see fig. 2.20). The Presets provide you with a library of designs to use as a starting point for your own creations. You can save your own designs as new presets, and you can delete presets as well. The Gradient Designer ships with 17 categories of presets containing over 300 presets.

FIGURE 2.19

The KPT test preview images.

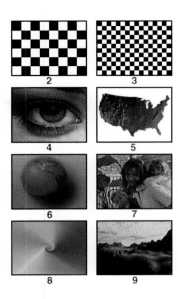

FIGURE 2.20

The Gradient Designer presets.

When you save a preset, most of the settings and parameters in the extension user interface for the current design are saved. Each preset is given a descriptive title that somehow relates to the gradient design contained within. The presets that ship with KPT have some fairly wild and sometimes obscure titles. Try loading different ones at random to get a feel for how their naming conventions relate to the given design.

Each of the major KPT extensions have associated presets. These presets are saved in an external file. For the Gradient Designer, this file is "Factory Presets" on the Mac, and KPT_ORIG.GRD in Windows. It exists in the same folder or directory with the other KPT plug-in files. By default, new presets that you create are stored in this file. To add a new preset, follow these steps as demonstrated in the Gradient Designer:

1. Start the Gradient Designer extension.

2. Create your gradient design.

3. Click on the Add button next to the Presets window. The Save Gradient As dialog box appears in the center of your screen, and contains both an input box for the preset name, and two pop-up menus for selecting categories or hub files (see fig. 2.21).

By default, the new preset is saved to the Misc. category. If you want to save to a different category, click and hold on the button to the right of the Category label. Then drag the cursor to choose a category for the preset file. You can create a new category by selecting the Add a New Category option, and then typing the new name for the category and clicking on OK. This returns you to the Save Preset As dialog box. You can create up to 64 categories with no limit on the number of presets contained in each category.

4. Type the name of your new preset. Then click on OK.

The new preset now should appear in the presets list along with the existing presets of the same category. You now can load the new preset at any time, just like the factory presets.

You also can create your own separate hub files. These files act as external libraries of presets. Each extension can support up to five hub files. On the Mac, KPT comes with a Factory Presets hub file, and a User Presets hub file. To create a new custom hub on the Mac, just copy the User Presets file and rename it. It will now appear along with the other preset hub files.

In the Windows Gradient Designer, hub files have a .GRD file extension, and exist in the same directory with the rest of the KPT plug-ins. There is a different hub file for the Gradient Designer/ Gradients on Paths (.GRD), Texture Explorer (.TEX), and Fractal Explorer (.FRX). To create a new hub file in Windows, follow these steps:

1. Start the extension, create or choose a design, then click on the Add preset button. The Add Preset dialog box will appear.

2. At the top of the Add Preset dialog box, click and hold on the button next to the Preset Hub label.

FIGURE 2.21

The Save Gradient As dialog box.

3. Drag down to the Create New Preset File option and release.

4. The Add Preset dialog box changes, enabling you to type a name for the new hub file. This must be alphanumeric and contain no more than eight characters. Something like "MYHUB" works well.

Type in the new hub file name and click on OK.

5. You now can type the new preset name and it will be saved into the new hub file.

Now you have created a new hub file containing one preset. To save another preset into this new hub file, just repeat the Add process, but select the new hub file from the Preset File prompt before naming and saving the preset.

In Chapter 1, "Overview of KPT," you copied sample hub files from the accompanying CD-ROM to your plug-ins directory. These files are examples of external hub files for the extensions. When copied into the plug-ins directory, they automatically become part of the extension presets the next time the extension is launched.

The external preset hubs make it possible for you to create custom libraries of presets. These are portable and can be shared with other users on the same operating system platform, a handy feature for teams of graphic artists who need to stay in sync.

To delete a preset gradient, load the preset and click on the Del button (next to the Add button). This will generate the Delete Preset dialog box.

The purpose of the Delete Preset dialog is to make sure that you really want to delete the preset. If you click on YES, the gradient preset is deleted. If you click on NO, the operation is canceled. A message in the dialog box states that if you click on YES, the operation cannot be undone. The gradient attributes, however, stay present after you delete the preset, enabling you to recover an inadvertently deleted preset if necessary.

The Cancel and OK Buttons

The Cancel and OK buttons (refer back to fig. 2.1) enable you to exit from the current KPT extension. The Cancel button quits the extension without saving any changes you have made, and returns you to the parent application without applying your designs to the current image or selection. The OK button confirms your final design, quits the extension, and applies your design to the current image or selection.

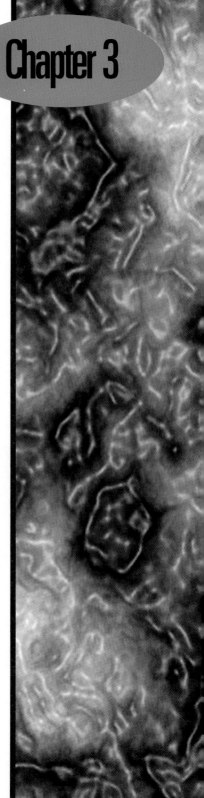

Chapter 3

The Gradient Designer

$\mathscr{B}$efore KPT, designing complex gradients or gradients that followed intricate feathered paths was a laborious process usually requiring precise painting or airbrushing techniques. The Gradient Designer makes it possible to generate these complex gradients with extreme control and reproducibility.

The Hub of the KPT Universe

The Gradient Designer is the core of the KPT extension set. Its primary purpose is designing gradients, ranging from simple to extremely complex. The Gradient Designer can be used alone, or in conjunction with the Gradients on Paths, Texture Explorer, or Fractal Explorer extensions. The Gradient Designer provides these other extensions with color and transparency information to use in generating their respective designs.

To start the Gradient Designer, follow these steps:

1. Start the KPT-compatible application (for example, Photoshop).

2. Open a new blank document in RGB color mode.

3. Locate the Gradient Designer in the plug-in filters section of your paint program and select it to launch the KPT interface.

When launched, the Gradient Designer window will appear on your screen (see fig. 3.1).

The interface controls enable you to load and modify the preset gradients, or create your own from scratch. KPT ships with a large number of presets that span a wide range of gradient designs, from simple to complex. These presets are an excellent starting point for the creation of new designs as well.

The Preset Menu

The Preset menu displays a list of categories that contain preset or predesigned gradients (see fig. 3.1). Hold the left mouse button down to move up or down on the category list to display the contents of each category. The gradient presets in each category have names that refer to the pattern contained within.

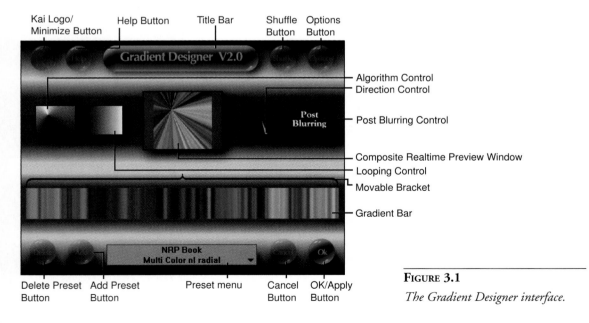

FIGURE 3.1

The Gradient Designer interface.

To call up a preset, perform the following steps:

1. Click and hold in the Preset Menu box in the bottom center of the Gradient Designer window.

2. Drag the cursor down the list to choose a category, then continue to drag inside the presets list until you find the preset you want.

3. Let go of the mouse button while the cursor is on top of the preset name to select that preset.

The preset gradient will then become the active gradient. To select another preset, repeat this process.

Designing Simple Gradients

Understanding how the Gradient Designer works requires a fundamental understanding of how a simple gradient is created. The following section demonstrates how a simple two-color ramp can be created in the Gradient Designer.

The Gradient Bar

In the center of the Gradient Designer interface is a long horizontal bar called the Gradient Bar (see fig. 3.2). The Gradient Bar functions as both a three-part window that displays the current

gradient's characteristics, and a control that activates the Pop-up Color Picker.

NOTE *See the sections later in this chapter for more information on the three-part Gradient Bar and the Pop-up Color Picker.* •

To see how this functionality works, design a simple gradient by performing the following steps:

1. Open a new document in RGB mode.

2. Start the KPT Gradient Designer.

3. Choose the All Clear preset from the NRP Book category. This preset contains absolutely no color information, and is equivalent to pressing Ctrl+X with the entire gradient selected.

NOTE *Make sure you've copied the NRP Book hub files from the accompanying CD-ROM HUB folder/directory to the Plug-Ins folder/directory used by your host plug-in compatible application. These hub files contain presets used in this text, and can be used as a reference point for examples provided here.* •

4. Once the preset is loaded, click and hold in the center of the left-most part of the Gradient Bar. This activates the Pop-up Color Picker, which appears below the Gradient Bar (see fig. 3.3).

FIGURE 3.2

The three-part Gradient Bar.

5. Continue to hold down the mouse button, drag the cursor into the color spectrum to select a color, and release the mouse button. The left part of the Gradient Bar now should display the chosen color, which fades off into transparency toward the right part of the Gradient Bar.

6. Repeat the process, but this time click in the right-most part of the Gradient Bar. Choose a different color from the color you chose for the left part of the gradient.

You now have created a simple gradient that ramps between the two colors chosen with the Pop-up Color Picker (see fig. 3.4).

To apply your newly created gradient to your image, click on OK in the lower right corner of the Gradient Designer window. The Gradient Designer will apply the new gradient to the underlying image using the Normal Apply mode.

Now that you've seen the basics of what the Gradient Designer can do, take a look at the controls in greater depth.

FIGURE 3.3
The Pop-up Color Picker.

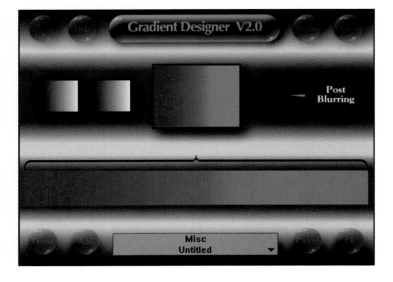

FIGURE 3.4
A simple two-color gradient.

The Gradient Designer Controls

The following section provides information about each control in the Gradient Designer interface. These controls enable you to manipulate all the parameters or characteristics of the gradient design. The Gradient Designer controls are as follows:

◆ The Algorithm Control

◆ The Looping Control

◆ The Realtime Preview window

◆ Direction Control

◆ Post Blurring

◆ The Movable Bracket

◆ The Gradient Bar

◆ The Pop-up Color Picker

Algorithm Control

The Algorithm Control is the left-most box in the group of five boxes that lie beneath the Title Bar.

These algorithms control the way a gradient is drawn, and range from straight linear blends to geometrically shaped bursts.

The Algorithm Control box displays the current gradient algorithm using a grayscale representation. This representation gives you a visual cue as to which algorithm is in use by displaying a pattern that corresponds to the algorithm. The following 10 algorithms are available for use (see fig. 3.5):

◆ Linear Blend

◆ Circular Sunburst and Elliptical Sunburst

◆ Radial Sweep

◆ Square Burst and Rectangular Burst

◆ Angular Shapeburst and Circular Shapeburst

◆ Angular Pathburst and Circular Pathburst

FIGURE 3.5

Algorithm Control menu.

Linear Blend

Linear Blend is a classic style that ramps between the colors along a linear or straight path (see fig. 3.6). This algorithm also is found in Photoshop's Gradient Fill function.

Circular Sunburst and Elliptical Sunburst

The Circular Sunburst is another popular gradient style that ramps between the colors in a circular, concentric manner. This algorithm also can be found in Photoshop's Gradient Fill function, known as a Radial type fill.

The Elliptical Sunburst is similar to the Circular Sunburst except that it uses an ellipsoidal shape (see fig. 3.7). It follows the aspect ratio of the image or selection, tailoring the ellipse to fit.

Radial Sweep

The Radial Sweep algorithm ramps the colors around a 360 degree arc from a central point (see fig. 3.8). This algorithm is useful for creating sun-like rays emanating from a specific point.

Square Burst and Rectangular Burst

The Square Burst and Rectangular Burst algorithms are like their Circular/Elliptical Sunburst counterparts, but use a square or rectangular shape for their respective shapes (see fig. 3.9). The

FIGURE 3.6
Linear Blend.

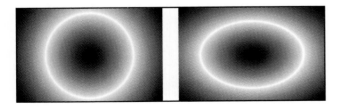

FIGURE 3.7
Circular Sunburst and Elliptical Sunburst.

Rectangular Burst follows the aspect ratio of the current image or selection.

The Rectangular Burst, when used with transparency, is a great tool for creating framing effects for an image. Framing effects create a mock frame around the interior of an image or selection. This type of effect is pretty common and usually involves multiple steps. Using the Rectangular Burst with transparency, however, performs this operation in one quick pass.

Shapeburst and Pathburst Algorithms

The Shapeburst and Pathburst algorithms enable you to create gradients that follow the contours of a selection (see fig. 3.10). The Shapeburst algorithm will fill the interior of a selection with a gradient. This is a great tool for filling the interior of complex selections with a gradient that closely follows the contours of a selection's edges.

The Pathburst algorithms create a gradient that follows the interior and the exterior of a selection. The outermost edges of the gradient on the outside of the selection fill an imaginary box surrounding the selection. Known as a bounding box, this imaginary rectangle surrounds the outermost edges of your selection.

FIGURE 3.8
Radial Sweep.

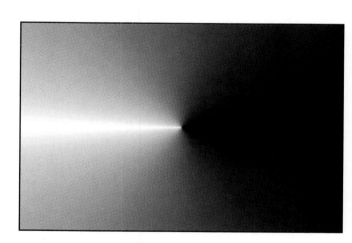

FIGURE 3.9
Square Burst and Rectangular Burst.

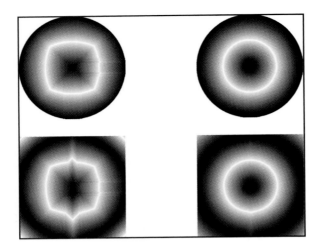

FIGURE **3.10**
Shapeburst and Pathburst.

Interestingly, the Shapeburst algorithms ignore any feathering attributes of a selection, filling from the edge of the marching ants boundary inward. In contrast, the Pathburst algorithms honor the feathering attribute, and feather on the inside and outside of the selection. The Pathburst's bounding box will extend to the edges of the selection's feathering, resulting in a fill that extends beyond the selection's edge by the number of pixels specified in the Feathering dialog box.

NOTE *For more information on selections, feathering, and marching ants, see the section, "KPT Fundamentals and Concepts" in Chapter 1.* ●

The Shapeburst and Pathburst algorithms come in two flavors, Circular and Angular. The Circular burst is a softer, rounded, smooth fill, while the Angular burst is a harder, sharp-edged fill.

The Looping Controls

The Looping Control menu (see fig. 3.11), located between the Algorithm Control and the Preview windows, enable you to control how a gradient design repeats itself. The three main loop parameters are as follows:

◆ Waveform Type

◆ Distortion

◆ Repetition

The Looping Control box displays the current attributes of your looping parameters in a graphical representation. This representation visually depicts the current settings in all three looping categories.

Waveform Type

Waveform Type enables you to choose how the gradient repeats itself, also known as a *waveform* (see fig. 3.12). The first waveform, known as

FIGURE **3.11**

The Looping Control menu.

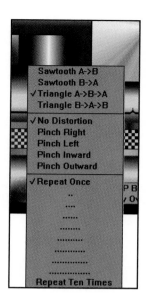

sawtooth, loops the gradient from beginning to end, then starts again from the beginning. The visual representation of the sawtooth waveform looks like a tooth on a cutting saw. The Sawtooth A->B and Sawtooth B->A settings sweep the gradient once from beginning (A) to end (B), or from the end to the beginning respectively. Both of these waveforms function as a single loop.

Another looping waveform, known as triangular, sweeps the gradient from beginning to end to beginning again. The visual representation of this waveform is a triangular shape. The Triangle A->B->A setting sweeps the gradient from beginning (A) to end (B) and back to the beginning (A), making B the midpoint of the sweep. Triangle B->A->B functions the opposite, making A the midpoint of the sweep.

Distortion

Distortion enables you to distort or "pinch" the entire gradient. This alters the gradient's linearity and skews the gradient in a particular direction (see fig. 3.13).

Distortion's Pinch Right and Pinch Left options pull the gradient to the right or left. The Pinch Inward and Pinch Outward options pull the gradient toward the center or the sides. The effect that results is a compression of the gradient toward the selected bias, appearing to "pinch" the gradient.

Repetition

Repetition enables you to control how many times the gradient repeats inside its given algorithm. You can choose to repeat from 1 to 10 times (see fig. 3.14). This function multiplies the chosen waveform by the number of repeats, creating a compound waveform.

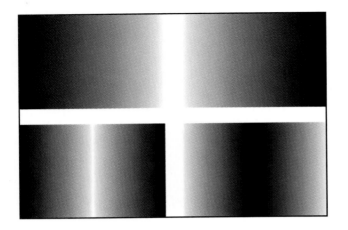

FIGURE **3.12**

Waveform.

FIGURE **3.13**

Distortion.

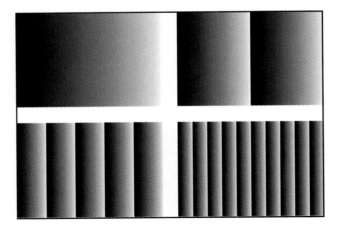

FIGURE **3.14**

Repetition.

Realtime Preview Window

The Realtime Preview window is common to all of the KPT extensions, but has slightly different functionality in each (see fig. 3.15). In the Gradient Designer, the Realtime Preview window has features specific to gradient previews, and enables you to see the following:

◆ The current gradient design

◆ The interaction between the current gradient design and the underlying image or test preview image

◆ The effects of any changes in the gradient's parameters performed in the Gradient Designer

The Realtime Preview Linking mode is toggled on and off by selecting the Realtime Linking option from the Options menu. When the option has a check mark next to it, the Realtime Linking option is activated and any change you make in the extension is immediately updated. If it is not checked, the window is not updated until after you perform a change. Leaving the Realtime Linking option off is sometimes useful for slower machines or to generally speed up things.

The Realtime Preview window also enables you to position the origin of the gradient for the Circular Sunburst, Elliptical Sunburst, Radial Sweep, Square Burst, and Rectangular Burst algorithms. Just click in the Realtime Preview window and drag to change the location of the center of the gradient. You can shift-click to snap the origin to the center, corners, or sides of the Realtime Preview window.

NOTE *To see the underlying image or test preview image at anytime, click in the Gradient Designer interface in any open area not occupied by a button or control.* ●

Direction Control

The Direction Control is located just to the right of the Realtime Preview window. This control enables you to set the direction of the Linear and Radial Sweep style gradients. It functions similarly to setting the hands on a clock. Click in the window and drag the control around the center to set the desired angle (see fig. 3.15).

The direction angle is represented by a vector emanating from a central point extending outward. This vector can be rotated 360 degrees, and the current angle setting is displayed underneath the Direction Control window in a small text box. Holding down the Shift key while selecting direction constrains the direction to 45 degree increments and exact points in corners.

Post Blurring

The Post Blurring control is the right-most box in the row of five boxes underneath the Title Bar. Post Blurring applies a blur effect to the gradient design ranging from 0 percent (sharp) to 100 percent (really blurry). The Post Blurring control displays a visual representation of the degree of blur, using the words "Post Blurring" as a preview image (see fig. 3.15).

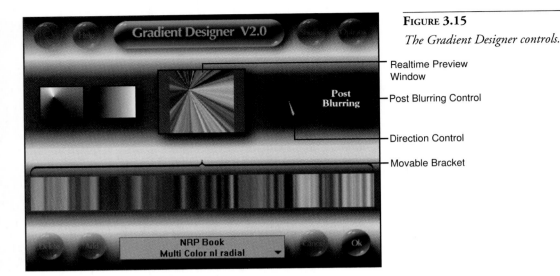

FIGURE 3.15

The Gradient Designer controls.

Realtime Preview
Window

Post Blurring Control

Direction Control

Movable Bracket

Clicking and dragging to the right will increase the amount of blur. Clicking and dragging to the left will decrease the amount of blur. The percentage value is displayed in a small text box underneath the Post Blurring control.

Once you have dialed up a Post Blur percentage, you can optionally apply it to the Gradient Bar by clicking once in the Post Blur box. This actually will blur the colors in the entire Gradient Bar, and is not affected by the size or position of the Movable Bracket.

NOTE *Use the Shuffle menu described in Chapter 2 to randomly shuffle the parameters. By shuffling with one or more parameters disabled you can quickly get a sense of how different schemes produce different results. For example, shuffle the Looping and Algorithm only to view the possibilities of a certain gradient color scheme.* ●

The Movable Bracket

The Movable Bracket is a powerful tool for making precise selections inside the Gradient Bar. Think of it like the Marquee tool in Photoshop; it enables you to make precise selections within the Gradient Bar that then can be altered or deleted. The Movable Bracket is the cornerstone of complex gradient design, enabling you to precisely control placement, color, and transparency within a given selection.

The Movable Bracket works with the Gradient Bar to define the active area for creating blends or performing operations within the Gradient Bar. It consists of two end points and one middle point (see fig. 3.15). You can move the end points by clicking on either one and dragging right or left. To move the entire bracket at once, click-and-drag on the middle point. The Movable Bracket size can be adjusted symmetrically by pressing Ctrl and clicking on the middle point and dragging up or down.

By default, the Movable Bracket spans the entire Gradient Bar, and the entire gradient will be affected by any gradient blends or transformations. If reduced to a smaller width, only the active area between the end points of the bracket is affected. This enables you to create complex gradients with multiple colored and transparent sections. Tools available to you for editing gradients include the Cut (Ctrl+X or ⌘+X), Copy (Ctrl+C or ⌘+C), Paste (Ctrl+V or ⌘+V), Flip (Ctrl+F or ⌘+F), and Invert (Ctrl+I, Windows only) commands. In this case, however, KPT uses its own Clipboard buffer, leaving the system Clipboard buffer unaffected. To use the editing commands, follow these steps:

1. Position the Movable Bracket over the desired area (see fig. 3.16).

2. Press ⌘+X (Mac) or Ctrl + X (Windows) to cut, and then press ⌘+C (Mac) or Ctrl+C (Windows) to copy (see fig. 3.17).

3. Move the bracket to a new location and press ⌘+V (Mac) or Ctrl+V (Windows) to paste the gradient you cut in step 2 into the current active area (see fig. 3.18).

4. To flip the colors in the Gradient Bar, press ⌘+F (Mac) or Ctrl+F (Windows) to flip the gradient within the active area (see fig. 3.19). Flipping also lets you manually position pieces of a gradient similar to the A->B->A looping waveform by copying the original, then pasting and flipping a copy adjacent to the original.

FIGURE 3.16

Position the bracket over a specific area.

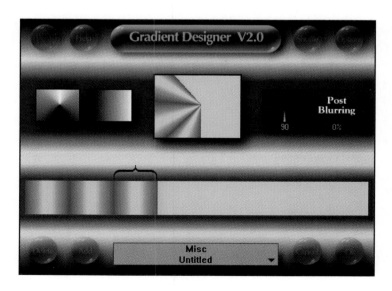

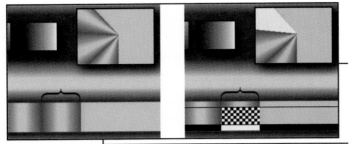

FIGURE 3.17

Copy or cut the selected area.

Cut

Copy

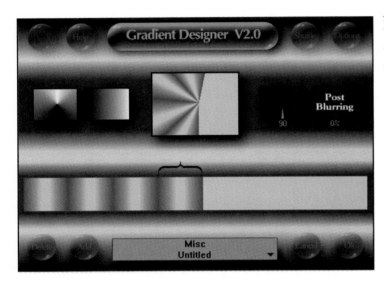

FIGURE 3.18

Move the bracket and paste copied area to new location.

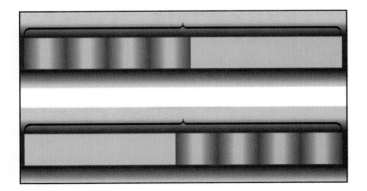

FIGURE 3.19

Flip the entire gradient within the Movable Bracket area.

Whenever you use the Cut command, it clears the active area defined by the Movable Bracket and leaves it 100 percent transparent or clear. This will reveal a bright black-and-white checkerboard pattern in the center of the Gradient Bar, indicating that this area is at 100 percent transparency.

NOTE *If you cut or copy a large active area and proceed to paste it to a smaller active area, KPT will automatically compress or shrink your selection to fit in the smaller space. Likewise, if you cut or copy a small active area and proceed to paste it to a larger active area, the selection will be stretched larger to fit. This feature enables you to design an area of the gradient on a larger scale, then paste it into a small area.* •

Figure 3.20 demonstrates some of the ways the Movable Bracket tool can be used to create various gradients.

The Three-Part Gradient Bar

The Gradient Bar is made up of three parts, and is also known as the three-part Gradient Bar (see fig. 3.21). It is the long horizontal box directly beneath the Movable Bracket. It has multiple functions, and is the core control of the Gradient Designer extension.

Whenever you design a gradient in the Gradient Designer, you put together color and transparency elements. You have precise control over which areas of your gradient contain transparency information. The Gradient Bar's three parts enable you to independently control the application of color or transparency.

FIGURE 3.20

Creating gradients with the bracket.

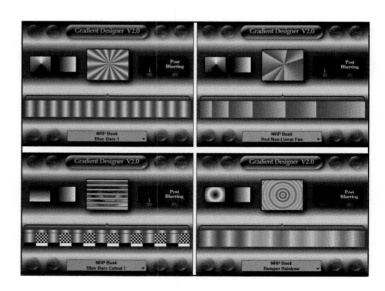

The Gradient Bar is divided into the following sections:

◆ The Color Gradient

◆ The Gradient Bar (color and transparency)

◆ Alpha Channel Gradient

The Color Bar displays the current color values used in the gradient, regardless of which parts contain transparency. It is represented as a thin horizontal strip at the top-most part of the Gradient Bar. It serves not only as a window that displays the gradient but also as an active selection area that enables you to grab color information from any preset gradient without affecting the transparency information.

The Opacity Bar works similarly to the Color Bar, but represents the degree of transparency as shades of gray. There are 256 shades of gray, with values ranging from 0 to 255, black being 0 (fully opaque) and white being 255 (fully transparent). The shades in between are partially transparent. Any area of the gradient that is transparent reveals an underlying black-and-white checkerboard image in the Gradient Bar. This enables you to visually judge how much transparency is being applied in specific areas of the gradient.

If the current gradient contains no transparency, the Opacity Bar is solid black from end to end, and the Color Bar looks identical to the Gradient Bar.

The Gradient Bar is represented as the wide strip in the center of the three-part Gradient Bar. It serves as both a window that displays the current gradient's color and transparency characteristics, and as an active selection area that activates the Pop-up Color Picker.

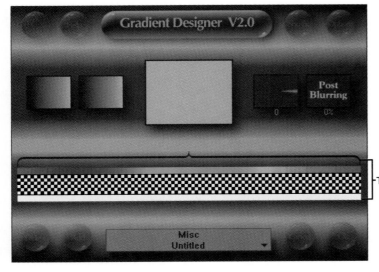

FIGURE 3.21

The three-part Gradient Bar.

Three-Part Gradient Bar

To see how these three bars work together in displaying the current gradient's characteristics, perform the following steps:

1. Start your KPT-compatible plug-in application, and open a new document in RGB mode.

2. Launch the Gradient Designer extension.

3. Load the All Clear preset from the NRP Book category (see fig. 3.22).

NOTE *Make sure you've copied the NRP Book hub files from the accompanying CD-ROM HUB folder/directory to the Plug-Ins folder/directory used by your host plug-in compatible application. These hub files contain presets used in this text, and can be used as a reference point for examples provided here.* •

In the All Clear preset, you can observe how the Opacity Bar is solid white, resulting in a 100-percent transparent gradient with no visible color information. The Color Bar still shows the original color information, in this case a warm hue color spectrum. None of these colors are actually visible, and as a result, the Gradient Bar shows the underlying checkerboard completely unobstructed.

4. Load the All Black preset from the NRP Book category (see fig. 3.23).

The All Black preset contains all black color information at 100-percent opacity. The resulting Color Bar, Gradient Bar, and Opacity Bar are all black.

5. Load the Real Red to Nowhere preset from the NRP Book category (see fig. 3.24).

FIGURE **3.22**

Loading the All Clear *gradient.*

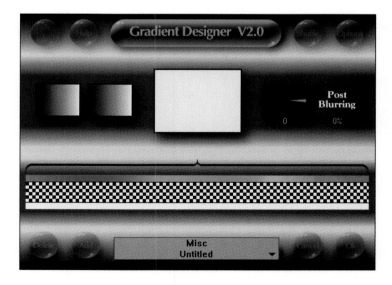

In figure 3.24, you can see that the Color Bar is bright red, and the Opacity Bar sweeps left to right from black to white. The resulting gradient begins as solid red, then fades to 100-percent transparency as the corresponding opacity values transition to white.

The Pop-Up Color Picker

The Pop-up Color Picker is a crucial component in the gradient design process. It enables you to choose colors from a variety of 24-bit color spaces that will be included in your gradient. You can have over 500 colors within a single gradient. The

FIGURE 3.23

Loading the All Black *gradient.*

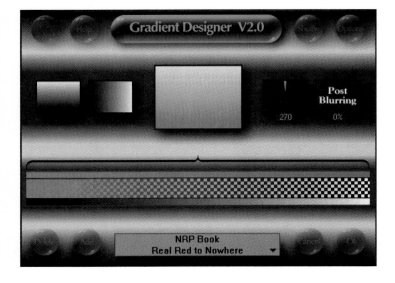

FIGURE 3.24

Loading the Real Red to Nowhere *gradient.*

Pop-up Color Picker is activated when you click and hold anywhere in the active area of the Gradient Bar section of the three-part Gradient Bar. This action changes the mouse pointer to an Eyedropper tool (see fig. 3.25). You can drag the Eyedropper tool anywhere in the color spectrum or on-screen, and then release the mouse button to select a color.

The Pop-up Color Picker enables you to select colors within several different color spectrums, described as *color-space slices*. These color-space slices are cross-sections of different color spectra, including spectrums like saturated and unsaturated, CMYK, and other color space models. By default, the Gradient Designer uses an RGB/HSV spectrum, enabling you to select from over 400 hues with 40 shades of intensity in one quick operation. This is much more powerful than color-picking schemes provided with your operating system, which operate in a two-dimensional color space.

NOTE *The placement of the cursor while clicking in the Gradient Bar determines where the color is applied in the gradient. In addition, you can only select colors for a range that exists within the area defined by the Movable Bracket. Clicking outside the active area has no effect. When designing a gradient that starts with one specific color and transitions to another, make sure you click all the way to the left or right side of the Gradient Bar or active area. This ensures that your gradient starts and ends precisely using the colors you select.* ●

In figure 3.25 notice how the Color Picker is divided into different rectangular sections. These sections give you precise control over the application of color and transparency. In the center, a colorful band sweeps along a horizontal bar. This is the color swatch for the current spectrum. The color values change along a horizontal axis, and the intensity levels along a vertical axis. To see how this works, perform the following steps:

1. Click and hold in the Gradient Bar to activate the Pop-up Color Picker.

2. Drag the Eyedropper tool down into the color swatch, then drag slowly from left to right along the swatch (see fig. 3.26).

NOTE *Notice how the Red, Green, and Blue numerical values in the small boxes above the color swatch change as you drag the Eyedropper tool. This is how color values are selected. The Realtime Preview window also reflects the changes in color simultaneously (if the Realtime Linking option is checked in the Options menu).* ●

3. Stop at a specific color, then drag the Eyedropper tool up and down within the confines of the color swatch.

FIGURE 3.25

The Pop-up Color Picker.

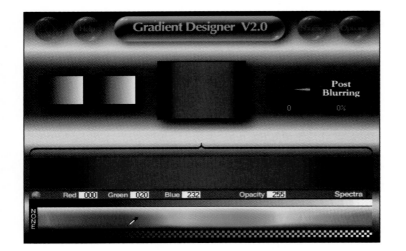

FIGURE 3.26

Choosing a color with the Eyedropper.

In figure 3.27, notice how the intensity of the chosen color increases as you near the top of the color swatch. Color intensity values are selected by moving the cursor vertically, which enables you to simultaneously adjust luminance or intensity values while selecting a color on a horizontal axis.

Choosing Shades of Gray

Directly above the Pop-up Color Picker's color swatch is a band of gray running from black to white along a horizontal axis. This swatch enables you to alternately choose from 256 shades of gray (see fig. 3.28). Drag along this bar from left to right and you will notice the RGB numerical values increasing in equal amounts.

FIGURE 3.27

Choosing a color's luminance by dragging the Eyedropper vertically.

FIGURE **3.28**

Choosing shades of gray with the Pop-up Color Picker.

Setting Transparency Levels

Directly below the color swatch is another thin horizontal box that enables you to adjust the level of transparency for the selected area. The values from left to right range from 0 percent to 100 percent transparent. Drag along this bar from left to right and notice how the gradient becomes more transparent. This is how you set transparency. On the left side of the color swatch is a box labeled NONE (see fig. 3.29). Drag over this box and it sets the opacity value to 0 or completely transparent.

A numerical readout labeled Opacity is to the right of the RGB readouts. This reflects the current level of transparency, ranging from 0 (completely transparent) to 255 (opaque).

Getting It to Work

The trick to getting predictable results with the Pop-up Color Picker is to understand the following concepts:

◆ The Eyedropper is live as soon as you click in the Gradient Bar. Anywhere you drag the Eyedropper after you click immediately affects the color in your gradient, even if you drag just a little bit. This makes it easy to inadvertently change the color if you accidentally stray with the cursor or try to just change opacity.

◆ The area containing the numerical readouts is neutral (see fig. 3.30). This area in the Pop-up Color Picker containing the numerical readouts for the Red, Green, Blue, and Opacity values is a place you can move the cursor without affecting the original gradient. Even if you've somehow changed the color, moving over this area will restore it to the original values.

You can press Esc at any time to abort the color picking operation and return to the original gradient.

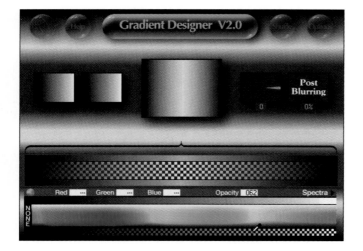

FIGURE 3.29

Setting transparency with the Pop-up Color Picker.

FIGURE 3.30

The numerical readouts area in between the three-part Color Bar and the color spectrum.

◆ Use the keyboard to alternately set transparency or to fill with a solid color. The keyboard enables you to select transparency to 10 different increments while choosing a color. The opacity scale is accessed by holding down the 0 to 9 keys while picking a color. The 0 key represents an opacity value of 000 or completely transparent. The 9 key represents an opacity value of 230, or nearly opaque. Holding down the Alt key while selecting color or transparency fills the entire active area with the color or level of opacity.

Other Keyboard Aids

You can modify the characteristics of your gradient with the aid of several other keyboard commands. Use these while clicking in the Gradient Bar:

◆ Hold down ⌘ (Mac) or Ctrl (Windows) while clicking and dragging in the Gradient Bar to slide or "rotate" the active area in the direction chosen. This enables you to move the entire gradient at once and position it to suit your taste.

- Windows users can hold down Ctrl+1, Ctrl+2, Ctrl+3, or Ctrl+4 while clicking and dragging to rotate the Red, Green, Blue, or Alpha channels respectively within the active area. This gives you individual channel control in a rotate operation.

- Hold down Option (Mac) or Alt (Windows) while clicking and dragging in the Gradient Bar to compress or expand the gradient over the active area. Like the Pop-up Color Picker's Eyedropper tool, the position of the cursor determines the origin of the effect, in this case where the compression of the gradient emanates from.

- Windows users can hold down Alt+1, Alt+2, Alt+3, or Alt+4 while clicking and dragging to compress or expand the Red, Green, Blue, or Alpha channels respectively over the active area. The position of the mouse pointer while clicking and dragging affects where the compression or expansion originates.

- Mac users can hold down the Shift key while dragging the Movable Bracket by the center handle. This moves the bracket by the width of the current selection.

- Press the left arrow and right arrow to move the Movable Bracket left one pixel or right one pixel. Hold down Shift while pressing an arrow key to move the Movable Bracket by the width of the current selection. These commands are extremely useful for precise selection manipulation.

- Left-Shift+mouse click to move the left side of the Movable Bracket to the position of the mouse pointer. Right-Shift+mouse click to move the right side of the Movable Bracket to the position of the mouse pointer.

As mentioned earlier in the Movable Bracket section, the standard Cut, Copy, and Paste commands (Ctrl+X, Ctrl+C, and Ctrl+V) work within the Gradient Bar and enable you to manipulate sections of the gradient. These commands utilize a Clipboard inside the Gradient Designer. In addition, the Flip (Ctrl+F or ⌘+F) and Invert commands (Ctrl+I, Windows only) let you flip the gradient section over or invert the colors, respectively.

NOTE *The Cancel function also can be executed by pressing the Esc key. This returns you to the parent application without saving or applying your changes.* ◆

The OK function can be executed by pressing the Enter or Return key. This will apply the gradient to the current image or selection.

The Gradient Designer Preferences Settings

The Preferences settings can be accessed by clicking on the Options menu and selecting Preferences from the bottom of the list. These settings control how the Gradient Designer first appears each time it is launched.

Two of these options, Load Normal Gradient and Load Smooth Gradient, will automatically load a new gradient into the Gradient Designer based on the current image or selection. The color selection is based on width of selection divided by 2. The Gradient Designer then reads pixel values on the center line. Colors at the very top and very bottom are not read.

The Load Normal Gradient From Image option displays all colors with sharp distinction between them. They do not interpolate from one to another, but rather stop and start.

Selecting Load Smooth Gradient From Image interpolates or smoothes the transition from one color to another. Use it when you want a softer version of the normal gradient load.

The Return to Previous State option remembers the settings in the Gradient Designer the last time you clicked on OK, and returns the Gradient Designer to the same state (last rendered gradient) the next time you launch it.

In the lower left corner of the Preferences dialog box is the Display Text Readouts box. This option controls whether you see numerical readouts in the Gradient Designer. These readouts include the rotation angle of the Direction Control and the blur percentage of the Post Blur. Turn off this option if you feel that these two numerical readouts violate the graphical purity of the Gradient Designer, or you feel them to be unnecessary. This option does not affect the numerical readouts in the Pop-up Color Picker for Red, Green, Blue, and Opacity values.

Designing Complex Gradients

The following section demonstrates a few different ways to use the tools in the Gradient Designer to create gradients. This section contains some case studies that you can work through step by step by using Photoshop or another plug-in compatible paint program.

Creating Multibar Gradients

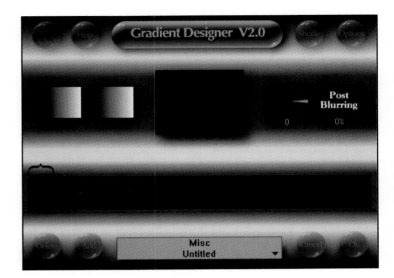

FIGURE 3.31

Load the All Black *preset. Make bracket small and align to the left side.*

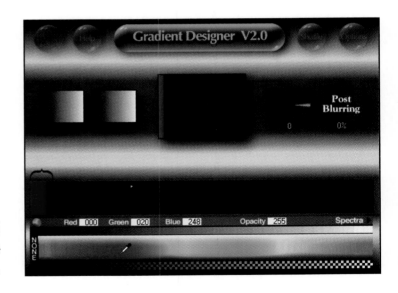

FIGURE 3.32

Set left side of selection area to dark blue.

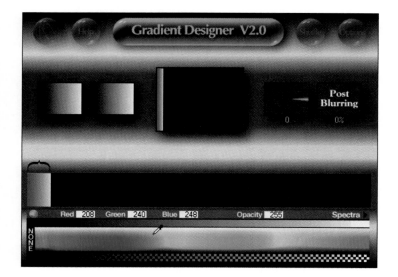

FIGURE 3.33

Set right side of selection area to light blue.

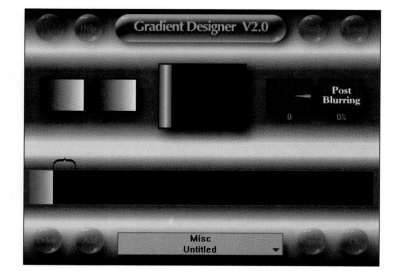

FIGURE 3.34

Copy and then move the section.

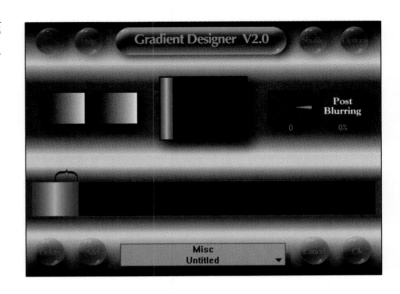

FIGURE 3.35

Paste and then flip the section.

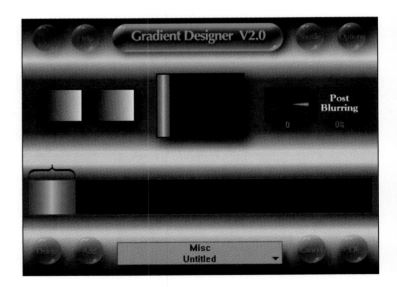

FIGURE 3.36

Position left side of bracket, then press
⌘+C or Ctrl+C to copy.

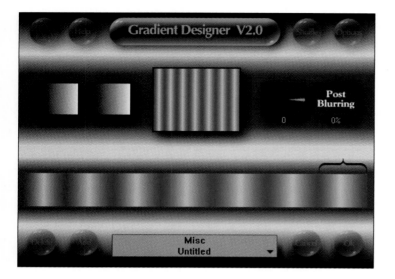

FIGURE 3.37

Move section, paste, and then repeat and align.

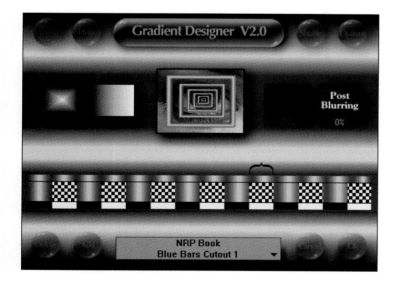

FIGURE 3.38

Load Blue Bars 2, *pinch left, and change to Rectangular Burst.*

FIGURE 3.39

Load Landscape*; add blur to horizon line by selecting area, then clicking in the Gradient Bar underneath.*

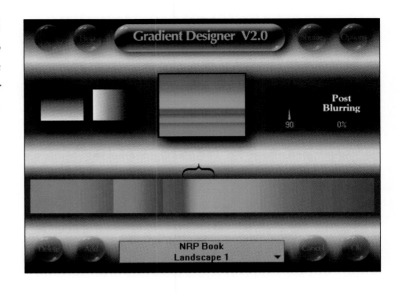

Creating Moire Art

FIGURE 3.40

Open new doc, load Blue Bars 1*, move origin, and click on OK.*

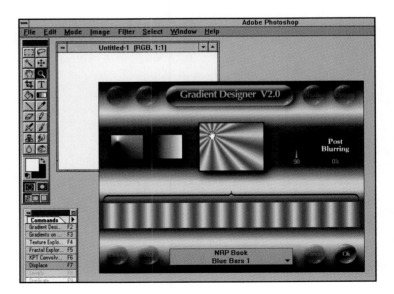

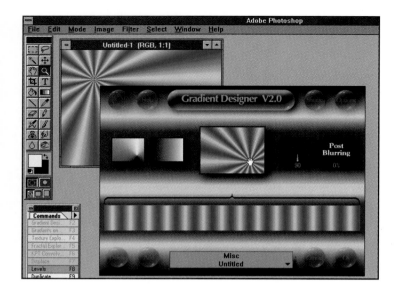

FIGURE 3.41

Restart GD, use same preset, and move origin to lower right.

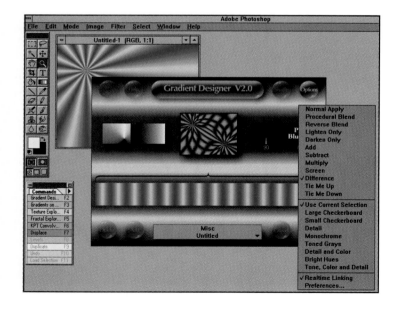

FIGURE 3.42

Select Difference Apply mode, and click on OK.

FIGURE 3.43

Moire art in action (final art).

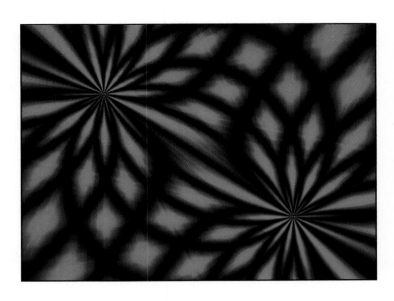

FIGURE 3.44

Open new doc, start GD, load Colored Rings, move origin to upper right, pinch left, and click on OK.

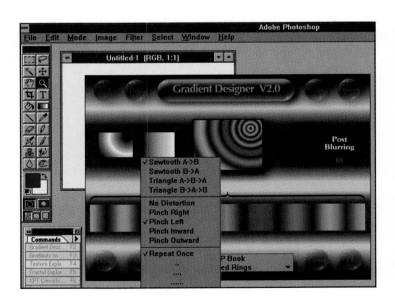

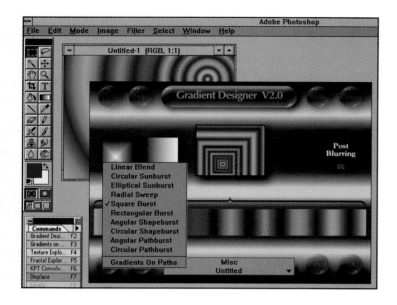

FIGURE 3.45

Restart GD, move origin to lower left, change to Square Burst, and press ⌘+F (Mac) or Ctrl+F (Windows) to flip.

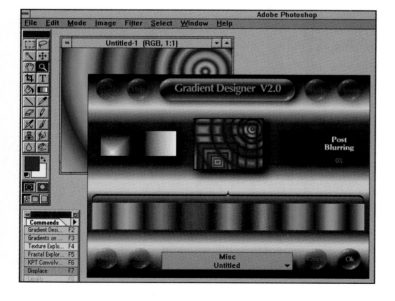

FIGURE 3.46

Select Darken Apply mode, then click on OK.

FIGURE 3.47

More moire art results (final image).

Using Shapeburst Fills

FIGURE 3.48

Create a number of different selections. Save the selections in an Alpha Channel.

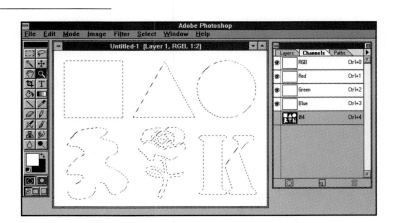

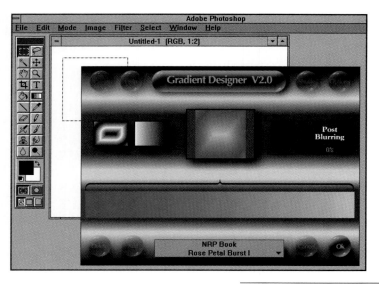

FIGURE 3.49

Load one selection, and fill with Shapeburst gradient from the Gradient Designer.

FIGURE 3.50

Fill all selections with Shapeburst gradient.

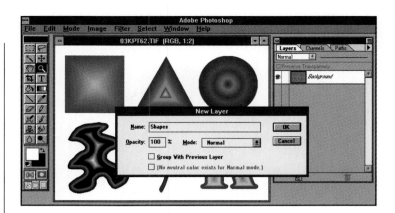

FIGURE 3.51

Create a new image layer.

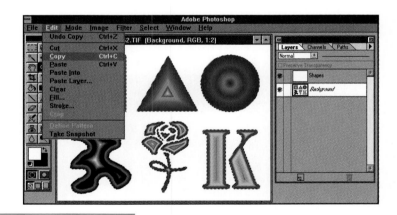

FIGURE 3.52

Load selections, and Edit/Cut to Clipboard.

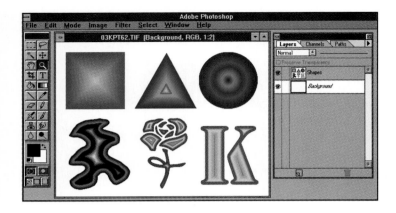

FIGURE 3.53

Select new layer, Edit/Paste the designs, then clear layer 1.

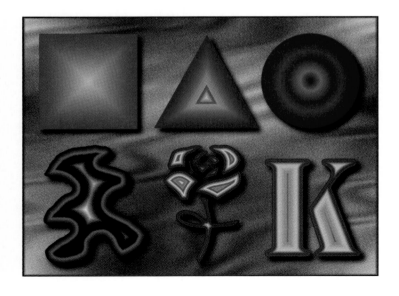

FIGURE 3.54

Add drop shadows and background texture to layer 1.

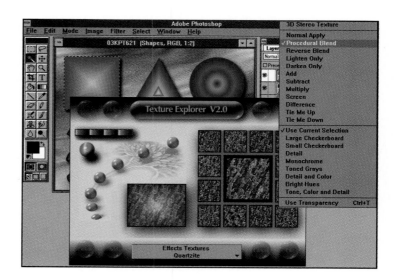

FIGURE 3.55

*Procedural Blend Texture Explorer
textures to selections in layer 2.*

FIGURE 3.56

The final results.

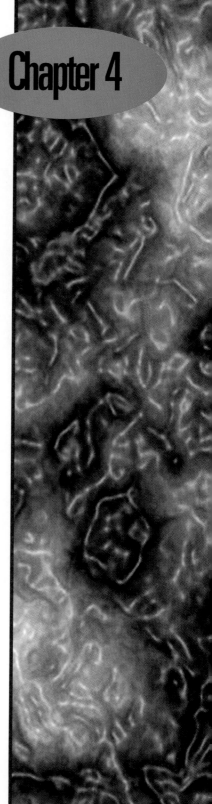

Chapter 4

Gradients on Paths

The KPT Gradients on Paths extension works hand in hand with the Gradient Designer. Gradients on Paths enables you to take your gradient designs and wrap them around a user-defined path. With this capability, you can create dazzling type effects and a variety of path-based special effects such as glows or halos around objects, clouds or fog effects, or shiny tubing. In this chapter, you'll explore this capability.

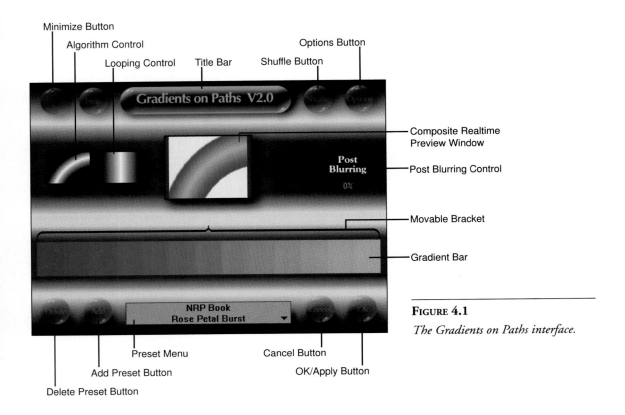

Minimize Button

Algorithm Control

Looping Control   Title Bar   Shuffle Button

Options Button

Gradients on Paths V2.0

Post
Blurring

0%

Composite Realtime
Preview Window

Post Blurring Control

Movable Bracket

Gradient Bar

NRP Book
Rose Petal Burst

Preset Menu   Cancel Button

Add Preset Button   OK/Apply Button

Delete Preset Button

FIGURE 4.1
The Gradients on Paths interface.

Taking Your Gradient Designs Down the Proverbial Path

The KPT Gradients on Paths extension applies a gradient design to a user-defined path or selection outline. For this to work, your plug-in compatible application must support paths or selections, with the capability to feather that selection to increase the outline width. Refer to Chapter 1, "Overview of KPT," for a more detailed description of programs that meet this requirement. If you attempt to start the extension in an application that does not support feathered selections, you will get an error message.

NOTE *For more information on selections and feathering, see the "KPT Fundamentals and Concepts" section in Chapter 1.* ●

Using Gradients on Paths

The Gradients on Paths extension is accessed by selecting it from your plug-in Filters menu, or by choosing the Gradients on Paths option from the Gradient Designer's Algorithm Control menu. Before you start the Gradients on Paths extension, however, you need to create a feathered selection in your plug-in compatible application. To do this, follow these steps as demonstrated in Photoshop:

1. Open a new document in RGB mode, 320×320 pixels in size.

2. Using Photoshop's Lasso or Marquee tools, create a selection path in the document (see fig. 4.2).

3. Feather the selection to a width of 10 pixels by choosing Select/Feather and entering a value of 10 in the dialog box (see fig. 4.3). Then click on OK.

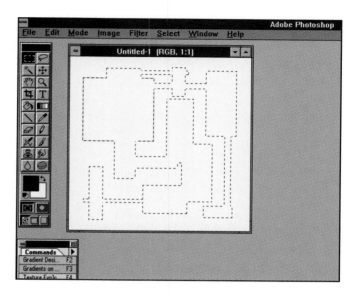

FIGURE 4.2

Creating a selection path.

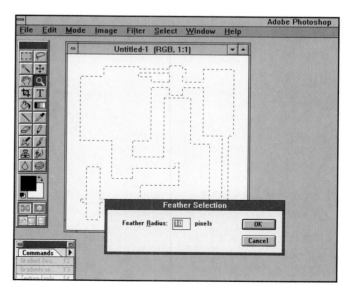

FIGURE 4.3

Feathering the path.

To see the Gradients on Paths extension at work, continue the steps as follows:

4. Launch the Gradients on Paths extension.

5. Load the Spectrum banded preset from the Basic Gradients category.

6. Click on OK to apply the gradient to your feathered selection (see fig. 4.4).

The preset then is applied to the feathered selection. This essentially "wraps" the gradient around the selection, using the marching ants as its centerpoint. The higher you set the feathering radius, the wider the gradient wrap will be. You need to make sure you specify at least 1 pixel feathering for the effect to be visible.

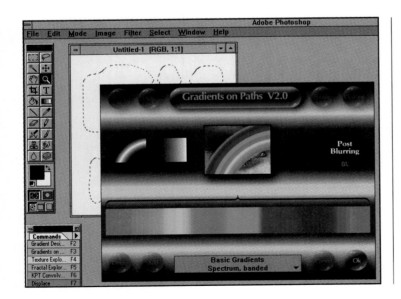

FIGURE 4.4

Applying a color gradient to the path.

Photoshop's Lasso and Marquee tools have built-in feathering settings. You can access these by double-clicking on the Lasso or Marquee tool icons, and entering a value into the Feather dialog box. Then draw the selection with the Lasso or Marquee tools and feathering automatically is applied.

The terms for selection and feathering might be different if you are using a plug-in compatible program other than Photoshop. In Fractal Design Painter 2, for example, the selection is known as a frisket.

NOTE *Refer to Chapter 1, "Overview of KPT," for more information on plug-in compatible programs.* ●

The Gradients on Paths Interface

As you might have noticed in figure 4.1, the Gradients on Paths interface is nearly identical to the Gradient Designer interface. Subtle differences exist in the Gradients on Paths interface that enable features specific to this extension.

NOTE *Refer to Chapter 3, "The Gradient Designer," for more detailed information about the Gradient Designer interface controls.* ●

The Preview Window is slightly different in that it does not preview the effects of the current gradient design on the actual selection, it shows the effects as applied to a sample curve. This is most likely due to the wide variability in the types of selections that are possible.

The sample curve in the Preview Window enables you to see how the current gradient design appears when applied to a curved path. By modifying the various gradient settings in the Gradients on Paths extension, you can see the effects of your changes immediately as applied to the curve. (Make sure that the Realtime Preview option is checked in the Options menu to enable Realtime Preview capability.)

Feathered Apply Modes

Another feature exclusive to the Gradients on Paths extension, known as the Feathered Apply Modes menu, is accessed by clicking and holding in the Preview Window. This menu gives you the option of picking which side of the path (inside or outside) the gradient appears, and whether to generate noise while rendering the gradient. Noise adds a speckled texture to the gradient, giving it the appearance of a hazy or grimy surface. The Feathered Apply Modes feature makes it easy to create glow outlines or halo effects around an object by specifying an "outside only" fill. An example of this is illustrated in figure 4.5.

FIGURE 4.5
Creating an object halo or glow using the Outside Only Apply Mode.

Noise Apply Mode

Another facet of the Feathered Apply Modes menu is the toggle called Noise Apply Mode. The Noise Apply Mode works in conjunction with transparency information contained in the gradient's Alpha Channel. Enable Noise Apply Mode by clicking and holding on the Preview Window to bring up the Feathered Apply Modes menu. Then select Noise Apply Mode (see fig. 4.6). When enabled, any transparent sections of the gradient will reveal random noise. The intensity of the noise effect varies depending on how dark the color is in the given gradient region. Use the Noise Apply option to create unusual textured borders that outline the gradient.

Figure 4.7 illustrates the effects of Noise Apply Modes with three different levels of Alpha in the gradient.

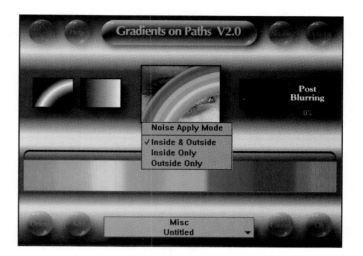

FIGURE 4.6

The Noise Apply Mode menu.

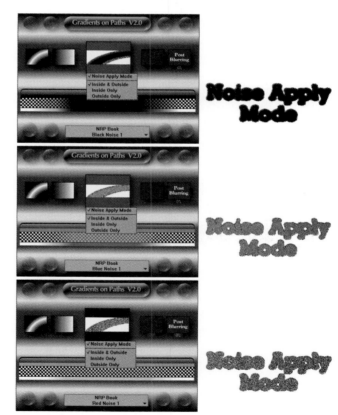

FIGURE 4.7

Varying degrees of gradient transparency used with the Noise Apply modes.

As you can see in figure 4.7, the intensity of the noise varies in direct proportion to the gradient's color and opacity settings. Where the gradient is less transparent or lighter in color, the noise is less noticeable. Conversely, increasing amounts of transparency and dark color increase the noise effect.

Looping Control, Post Blur, and Apply Modes

The Gradient Designer's Looping Control, Post Blur, and Apply Modes functions are built in to the Gradient's on Paths interface, and enable you to alter the gradient properties of your design.

The Looping Control alters the way in which your gradient design loops around the path. Change the settings for the Waveform, Distortion, or Repetition loops and see the effects on your path gradient. Changing the Waveform type to A->B->A will center the right side of your gradient along the path. Conversely, setting it to B->A->B will pull the end points of your gradient into the center of your path, similar to sliding your gradient halfway to one side.

The Post Blur setting blurs your gradient to blend the colors smoothly. This setting does not alter the path width or blur the edges, just the interior of the gradient.

The Apply Modes function enables you to alter the way your path gradient is applied to the underlying image. Try the Procedural Blend Apply mode to smoothly blend your path gradient in with the underlying image.

Figure 4.8 demonstrates some different combinations of control settings for Gradients on Paths.

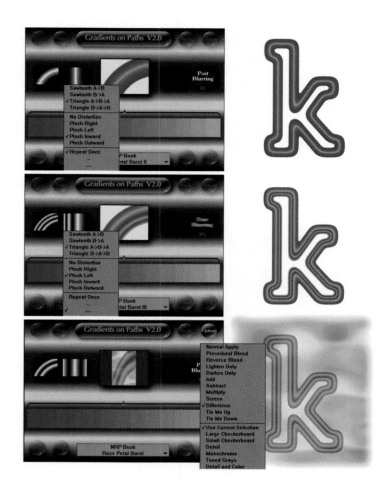

FIGURE 4.8

Various Gradients on Paths examples using different looping settings and apply modes.

Saving Presets

When you save a preset inside the Gradients on Paths extension, you are only saving information about the gradient, and not any Gradients on Paths-specific information. The only settings that are truly unique to Gradients on Paths are the Feathered Apply modes, which include the Inside/Outside and Noise Apply mode toggles. Unfortunately, the Feathered Apply menu settings are not saved.

Uses for Gradients on Paths

The following section contains illustrated examples of how to create several different practical designs using Gradients on Paths. Some of these are Photoshop-specific as they use Channel Operations to create the effects. If your plug-in compatible application supports Alpha Channels, you should be able to replicate these specific effects with equivalent commands.

Neon on a Brick Wall

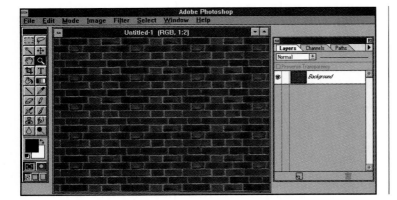

FIGURE 4.9

Open a new image, and fill the background with brick. Then create text selection, and save.

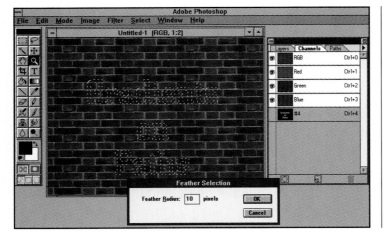

FIGURE 4.10

Load text selection, move down 10 pixels, and feather 10 pixels.

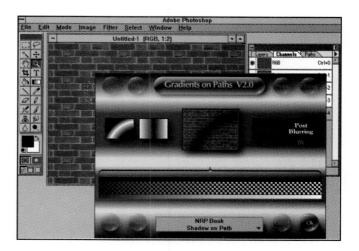

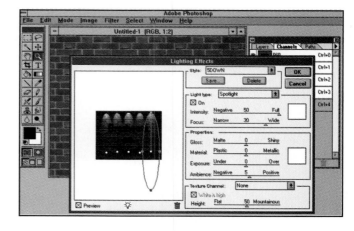

FIGURE 4.12

Adding rendered lighting effect to simulate down-lighting.

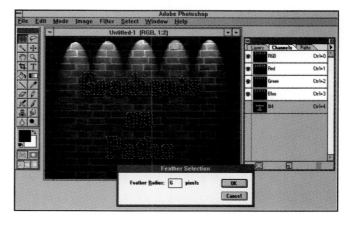

FIGURE 4.13

Load text selection, and feather 6 pixels.

FIGURE 4.14

Start Gradients on Paths, load Purple Neon, *and click on OK.*

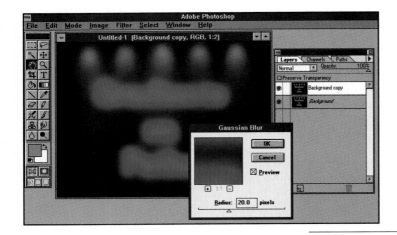

FIGURE 4.15

Copy background to a new image layer, and Gaussian Blur 20 pixels. Then change layer to Lighten Apply, 50 percent opacity.

FIGURE **4.16**

The final image.

Tubular Shapes

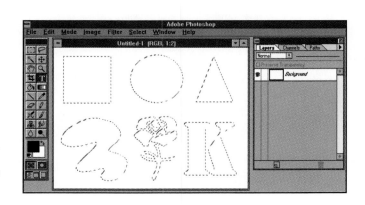

FIGURE **4.17**

*Create several selections and save in
an Alpha Channel.*

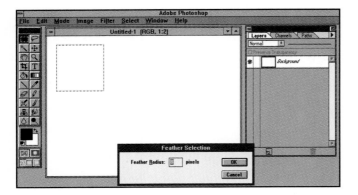

FIGURE 4.18

Load a selection, and feather 6 pixels.

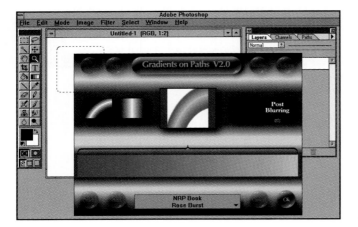

FIGURE 4.19

Start Gradients on Paths, load Rose Burst, *and click on OK.*

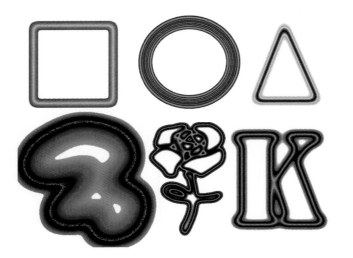

FIGURE 4.20

Try different feathering widths and gradient styles.

FIGURE 4.21

Add background and drop shadows.

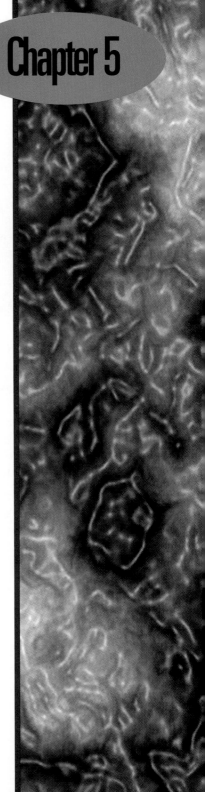

Chapter 5

The Texture Explorer

$\mathcal{T}$he Texture Explorer extension is perhaps the most useful of all the tools in the KPT collection. With the Texture Explorer, you can generate an almost unlimited variety of patterns and textures, useful for everything from 2D pattern fills to 3D texture maps (see fig. 5.1). These patterns can then be "rendered" to five predefined resolutions, or scaled to fit an entire selection or image. Use the Texture Explorer to generate conventional looks such as wood, metal, water, fire, clouds, and skies. Or, use it to create totally new, never-before-seen looks such as plasma energy, alien skin, or nuclear waste.

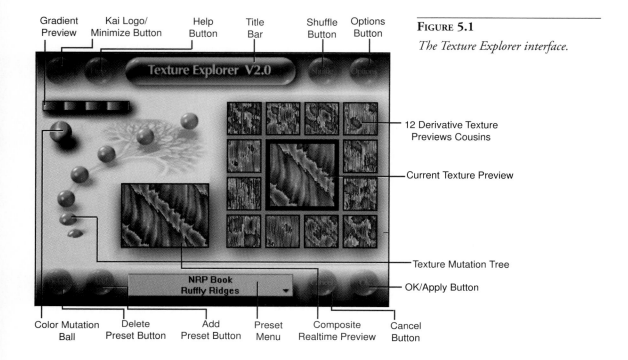

Gradient Preview — Kai Logo/Minimize Button — Help Button — Title Bar — Shuffle Button — Options Button

12 Derivative Texture Previews Cousins

Current Texture Preview

Texture Mutation Tree

OK/Apply Button

Color Mutation Ball — Delete Preset Button — Add Preset Button — Preset Menu — Composite Realtime Preview — Cancel Button

FIGURE 5.1

The Texture Explorer interface.

The Tool with the Widest Range of Uses

The Texture Explorer is distinctly different from the Gradient Designer and Gradients on Paths extensions because the bitmaps it produces are designed to repeat seamlessly when filled into a given area. This enables you to take a small rectangular texture and fill it into a larger area with no apparent edges where the adjacent tiles meet. What makes this Seamless Tiling feature possible is an advanced algorithm that automatically creates the given texture with tileable properties. This feature saves you multiple steps and provides a cleaner solution to tiling textures. Because the textures are stored as mathematical algorithms, considerably less disk space is required than storing the textures as bitmap image files.

If, however, you decide that you don't need a small tileable texture, you can use the Texture Explorer to create large textures up to extremely high resolutions. By default, these textures still have tileable properties, but even this feature can be disabled for creation of textures with non-tileable properties.

The interface design gives you the tools to start with a base texture, and then "mutate" it into a variant. HSC likes to use the analogy of genetics when describing the components of the Texture Explorer. In HSC terms, the user starts with the current texture, and mutates the genes into a derivative cousin. The degree or intensity of the mutation results in greater variation in the cousin. A small degree of mutation results in derivative cousins that are similar in appearance to the current texture. A large degree of mutation can produce derivative cousins that bear little or no resemblance to the current texture.

Besides mutating the textures, you have the capability of mutating the colors as well. With a direct link to the Gradient Designer, the Texture Explorer enables you to control pattern and color independently in the texture creation process. Any preset gradient can be called directly from the Texture Explorer and applied to the current texture, changing the colors. In addition, under Windows you can launch the Gradient Designer right from the Texture Explorer to create a custom gradient. Any changes made to the gradient in this mode are immediately updated in the Texture Explorer current texture window. This feature gives you immense control over texture colors.

As you explore new textures through the Texture Explorer's random creation functions, new random gradients are being generated as well. This can lead to color combinations never before seen, which can be captured and saved as preset gradients. In addition, all the apply modes from the Gradient Designer are in the Texture Explorer, enabling you to blend your texture design into an underlying image. This provides a third dimension beyond color and pattern to empower your texture creation abilities. And like the Gradient Designer, all of the textures you create in the Texture Explorer can be saved as presets to be used at a later time. Because the textures are stored as mathematical algorithms, considerably less disk space is required than storing the textures as bitmap image files.

Unraveling the Interface

The Texture Explorer's user interface consists of several controls and feedback windows that perform specific functions related to texture creation. Information about each of these components is provided in the following section.

The Current Texture Preview Window

On the right side of the Texture Explorer user interface is a large window surrounded by 12 smaller windows. This large window is known as the Current Texture Preview window (see fig. 5.2). In it you see the current texture design.

NOTE *On the Mac, the Current Texture Preview window has a tiny red ball in the upper left corner. This ball is known as the Enlarged Preview In Progress Light, and becomes red while the Current Texture Preview is being calculated.* •

Clicking and holding on the Current Texture Preview window produces the tiling menu. The tiling menu lets you specify what resolution or size (in pixels) you want to render the current texture. The choices are 96×96, 128×128, 256×256, 512×512, and 1024×1024 (see fig. 5.3). Additionally, you can select Tile Size of Selection, which will scale your texture design to fit edge-to-edge in the underlying selection or image. To choose a size, just drag and release over the selection to toggle it on. If the size you choose is smaller than the underlying image or selection, the texture will tile across and down starting in the upper left corner.

FIGURE 5.2

Current Texture Preview window.

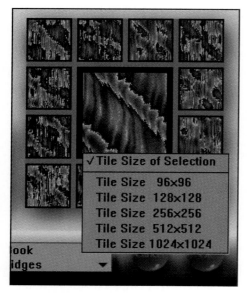

FIGURE 5.3

Tiling sizes menu.

you start the Texture Explorer. Always check the tiling sizes menu before you apply a texture to make sure that it's locked into the size you desire.

Derivative Cousins

Surrounding the Current Texture Preview window are 12 smaller windows that display its derivative cousins (see fig. 5.4). These cousins are random mutations of the current texture. Depending on the degree of mutation, these 12 windows may or may not resemble the texture in the Current Texture Preview window. Each time a texture is mutated through the Texture Explorer's controls, these

The default texture tiling size is 96×96 pixels. The tiling settings are reset each time you change the texture or load a new preset. They are not saved with the presets, nor are they retained the next time

12 windows will change to reflect the new derivative cousin.

To make a derivative cousin the current texture, click in the cousin's window and it will be swapped into the Current Texture Preview window. The previous current texture will be erased from memory.

Composite Realtime Preview Window

To the left of the Current Texture Preview window and the 12 derivative cousins windows is another window known as the Composite Realtime Preview window (refer to fig. 5.1). This window is similar to its counterpart in the Gradient Designer in that it displays the effects of the current texture in combination with its apply modes. When Normal Apply is chosen, the Composite Realtime Preview window is identical to the Current Texture Preview window. If the current texture's apply mode is anything but Normal Apply, or if the current texture contains transparency information, the Composite Realtime Preview window will reveal the underlying image blended with the current texture. The Composite Realtime Preview is updated in realtime whenever a change is made to the current texture or color gradient.

When you pass the cursor over the Composite Realtime Preview window, the arrow changes to a hand. If you click and drag inside the Composite Realtime Preview window, the placement of the current texture with respect to the underlying image is changed.

To see the effects of the tiling size in addition to the current texture and apply modes, click once quickly in the Current Texture Preview window. This changes it to a much larger version, and reveals the effects of all three attributes (texture, apply mode, and tiling size). This makes it easy to experiment with different apply modes and tiling sizes to get just the look you want. Click on the Enlarged Composite Realtime Preview window again to return to the Current Texture Preview window.

FIGURE 5.4

The 12 derivative cousins windows.

The Texture Mutation Tree

To the left of the Composite Realtime Preview window is a set of seven spheres arranged in an arc that floats over a graphic of a gray tree. These spheres comprise a set of controls called the Texture Mutation Tree (see fig. 5.5). The set of seven spheres represents seven levels of mutation ranging from slight (the bottom sphere, partially sunk into the ground) to great (the top sphere at the top of the tree). Clicking on one of these spheres mutates the current texture and generates 12 derivative cousins around the Current Texture Preview window. The higher the sphere is along the mutation tree, the greater the degree of mutation from the current texture.

When you see a cousin you like, click on its window to make it the current texture in the center window. Remember that doing this wipes out the previous texture that appeared in the Current Texture Preview window. You can undo one level of mutations by pressing Ctrl+Z, which will return the previous 12 cousins. Save any texture in the Current Texture Preview Window as a new preset to prevent losing something you like.

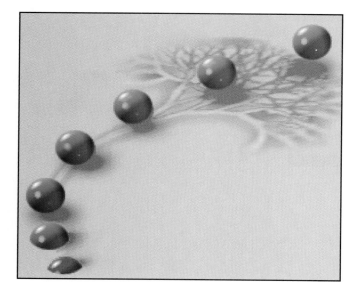

FIGURE 5.5

The Texture Mutation Tree.

You can lock in color information by pressing ⌘+L (Mac) or Ctrl+L (Windows). This is a toggle that maintains the current texture's color gradient information and enables you to mutate texture information only, without affecting color. Press ⌘+L (Mac) or Ctrl+L (Windows) again to return to the normal mutation mode.

While generating derivative cousins, you see several designs at once that you want to retain. This problem is addressed in a feature known as Texture Protection. By holding down the Option key (Mac) or the Alt key (Windows) and clicking on a derivative cousin window, you can "freeze" the mutation to prevent it from being changed by subsequent mutations. Frozen cousins have a red border around their window, as illustrated in figure 5.6. Once frozen, a derivative cousin is immune to changes generated by the Texture Mutation Tree function or by changing the textures color gradient.

FIGURE 5.6

Locking or "protecting" a cousin.

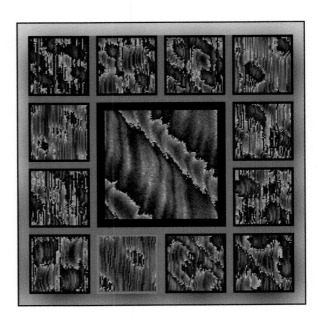

You also can apply Texture Protection to the Current Texture Preview window. If you choose a cousin while the center window is protected, the main window is swapped into a protected cousin window.

NOTE *In Windows, if you try to swap a protected cousin into the protected center window, you might lose the center window information.* •

TIP *HSC recommends always saving the Current Texture Preview window as a preset if you want to prevent losing the texture.* •

The Texture Explorer remembers protected windows and retains them each time you start the extension, regardless of whether you end up applying the texture with the OK button or exiting with the Cancel button.

The Color Mutation Ball

The colors that appear in the textures created with the Texture Explorer are based on gradients from the Gradient Designer. The Color Mutation Ball randomly rearranges the colors in the 12 derivative cousins without affecting the patterns, in essence creating new random gradients. This enables you to explore different color sets easily just by clicking on the Color Mutation Ball (refer back to fig. 5.1).

The Color Mutation Ball also randomly arranges other gradient properties such as alpha and looping. While this doesn't affect the pattern, it may have a drastic effect on the texture's appearance depending on how the new colors interact with the pattern.

In Windows, if you want to save the color information from the texture in the Current Preview window as a gradient, press Ctrl+G while in the Texture Explorer to launch the Gradient Designer. This brings in the color as a new gradient, which you can then save or modify at will. A texture's color information only exists in the left half of the Gradient Bar. Any color information appearing on the right half is ignored by the texture. By using the Gradient Bar's move (Ctrl+click-and-drag) and compress (Alt+click-and-drag) functions you can modify or position the gradient in the left half of the Gradient Bar in many different ways. You can manipulate the color information and render it back to the Texture Explorer's current texture by clicking on OK in the Gradient Designer. This returns you to the Texture Explorer and applies the modified gradient to the current texture.

NOTE *You can undo one level of color mutation by pressing Ctrl+Z.* •

The Gradient Preview Bar

Above the Color Mutation Ball is a strip of colors called the Gradient Preview Bar (refer back to fig. 5.1). This bar gives a visual representation of the texture's color gradient.

The Gradient Preview Bar also functions as a button that enables you to call up any Gradient Designer Preset as color information for the current texture. Click and hold on the Gradient Preview

Bar and the Gradient Designer Presets menu appears as illustrated in figure 5.7.

NOTE *In Windows, the Preset menu also includes an option to launch the Gradient Designer directly.* •

To choose a Gradient Designer Preset directly from the Texture Explorer, click on the Gradient Preview Bar and drag to select the desired category and preset from the menu. Alternately, you can use the left arrow or right arrow keys to ascend or descend through the Gradient Designer Preset hierarchy. Choosing a new gradient changes the texture's color information, replacing it with the preset gradient's color information. Calling a new gradient for a texture is distinctly different than using the Mutation Tree or Color Mutation Ball because it modifies the current texture and the derivative cousins, instead of just the cousins.

When you begin to understand the relationship between the Gradient Designer and the Texture Explorer extensions, you can start designing custom gradients for use as texture colors. Busy, multicolor, or complex color combinations result in very detailed textures, while smooth and subtle color changes in a gradient result in smoother less-detailed textures (see fig. 5.8).

Any portion of the left side of Gradient Preview Bar where abrupt color transitions occur will result in noticeable edges in the texture that follows the pattern's shape contours. Practice applying different gradient presets to a texture and watch how the colors in the gradient translate to the colors and patterns in the texture.

The Options Menu

The Options menu in the Texture Explorer is almost identical to its counterpart in the Gradient Designer (see fig. 5.9). For more information on the selection under the Options menu, refer to Chapter 2, "Unraveling the Interface." There are a few additional options, however, that appear that are specific to the Texture Explorer extension.

3D Stereo Noise Apply

When the 3D Stereo Noise option is checked in the Options menu, the current texture is used as the seed for a 3D Stereo Noise effect. While the 3D Stereo Noise Apply option is checked, you can still utilize the standard apply modes to apply the effect in a blended fashion.

```
    Texture Blends          ▶
    Basic Gradients         ▶
    Burst Gradients         ▶
    Complex Gradients       ▶
    Experimental Category   ▶
    Frames and Overlays     ▶
    Framing Effects         ▶
    Julia Set Gradients     ▶
    Laser Glow Gradients    ▶
    Metallic                ▶
    Misc                    ▶
    NRP Book                ▶
    New Gradient Examples   ▶
    Special Effects         ▶
    Strong Hues             ▶
    Surprises Galore        ▶
    Translucent             ▶
    Transparency Masks      ▶
```

FIGURE 5.7

Texture Explorer Preset categories.

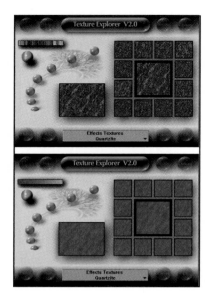

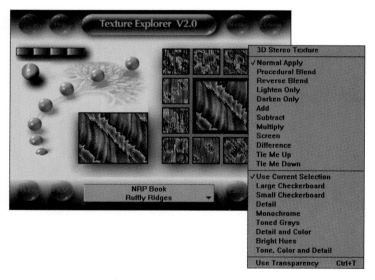

3D Stereo Noise creates a special dithered noise that, when applied, creates a stereo 3D image (see fig. 5.10). These images have become popular in recent years, and also are known as *stereograms*. A special dithering algorithm scrambles an image, then requires you to focus your eyes with a long convergence point to produce the 3D Stereo effect. See Chapter 8, "Other Filters and Utilities," for more information about the 3D Stereo Noise Apply filter.

FIGURE 5.10

3D Stereo Noise Apply mode.

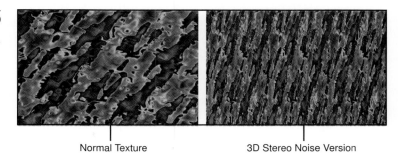

Normal Texture   3D Stereo Noise Version

Use Transparency

The Use Transparency option can be toggled on and off by selecting it from the Options menu, or by pressing ⌘+T (Mac) or Ctrl+T (Windows) while inside the Texture Explorer (see fig. 5.11). When activated, the Use Transparency option uses the corresponding texture gradient's Alpha Channel to create transparent areas in the texture. This enables the underlying image to show through wherever the texture gradient's Alpha Channel contains non-black values.

The Use Transparency setting is specific to the current texture or preset texture. If you save a texture preset with Use Transparency enabled it will stick and re-enable the next time the preset is loaded.

Global Transparency

You also can apply transparency globally (across the entire texture) by holding down one of the numeric keys 1-0 while clicking on the Texture Explorer's OK button. The numeric keys represent degrees of transparency, ranging from 1 (highly

FIGURE 5.11

Transparency in the gradient resulting in transparency in areas of the texture.

transparent) to 0 (fully opaque). Just hold down one of the numeric keys while clicking on OK, and the texture will render itself onto the underlying image using the degree of transparency you specify.

For example, hold down the 5 key while clicking the Texture Explorer's OK button to see the current texture applied to the underlying image at 50 percent transparency.

The Texture Explorer Presets

The preset functions in the Texture Explorer work in the exact same manner as in the Gradient Designer and Gradients on Paths extensions. Be sure to save a preset whenever you feel like you've discovered something interesting. Due to the immensely random nature of the texture generation, you might never see the identical texture again unless you save it as a preset.

You can use several keyboard shortcuts to select presets for the Texture Explorer. The up-arrow and down-arrow keys move to the previous or next preset, respectively. The PgUp and PgDn keys move to the previous or next category of presets (Mac users hold down the Option key first). The Home and End keys move to the first and last category of presets (Mac users hold down the Option key first).

The Equalizer

NOTE   *The Equalizer is a Windows-only feature.*   ●

For many years, audio professionals and home audio enthusiasts have used a device called an equalizer to fine-tune audio signal frequencies. The purpose of the audio equalizer is to compensate for acoustical deficiencies in the environment or alter the signal to suit a specific taste. KPT's Windows Texture Explorer has a function called the Equalizer that enables you to fine-tune the texture attributes like fine and coarse features, feature angles, detail levels, and diffusion. This tool was implemented in version 2.0 of KPT, and is a welcome addition that gives you even more control over texture creation.

The Equalizer can be started while in the Windows Texture Explorer extension by pressing Ctrl+E. This action produces a small user interface that floats to the left of the Texture Explorer user interface (see fig. 5.12). The Equalizer's user interface consists of two boxes containing small balls, a round blue button with two red lines, a vertical slider bar, and a horizontal slider bar. The user-interface can be repositioned by clicking and dragging it by the title bar and releasing in the new location.

Coarse Control

The square box at the upper left corner is known as the Coarse control. The "coarse" features of a texture refer to the larger, more dominant pattern characteristics. The Coarse control enables you to modify the coarse features in the current texture. The two sets of numbers at the bottom of the Coarse window reflect the current settings for the Coarse control, with larger numbers representing less pattern detail, and smaller numbers representing greater pattern detail. Just click-and-drag the control ball in the Coarse window to change the settings.

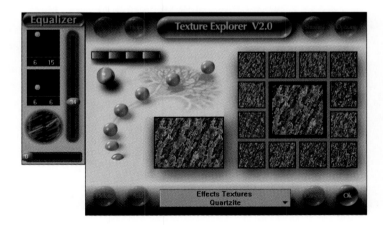

FIGURE 5.12

The Equalizer function.

Fine Control

The square box directly beneath the Coarse control is known as the Fine control. The Fine features of a texture refer to the smaller, less dominant pattern characteristics. The Fine control enables you to modify the fine or small details in the current texture. Like the Coarse control, the two sets of numbers at the bottom of the box reflect the current settings, with lower numbers representing greater pattern detail. Just click-and-drag the control ball in the Fine window to change the settings.

Angle Control

The blue button underneath the Coarse and Fine controls is known as the Angle control. The red indicator lines on each side control the X-Y axis of both the coarse and fine controls. The angle settings affect the texture's grayscale feature set, and result in what appears to be a "rotation" of the texture's pattern. Click-and-drag either of the red arrows up and down to modify the texture angles.

Detail Level

The vertical slider on the right side of the Equalizer is known as the Detail Level slider. Linked to the Coarse and Fine controls, the Detail Level slider increases or decreases the amount of detail in the current texture. Just click-and-drag the Detail Level slider up to increase the detail.

Diffusion Level

The horizontal bar at the bottom of the Equalizer is known as the Diffusion Level slider. Increasing the diffusion levels adds noise and washes or blurs the texture. Click-and-drag the Diffusion Level slider to the right to increase the amount of diffusion. See Chapter 7, "The Filter Effects," for a description of the Diffuse More filter, which performs a similar function on any bitmap.

Equalizer Modes

The Equalizer can operate in one of two modes. Earlier in this chapter you learned that the Texture Explorer generates algorithmically seamless tiling textures that, when tiled adjacently, create the illusion of one seamless bitmap. This mode is known as Constrained mode, where the texture is constrained to a tileable algorithm. The Equalizer enables you to work in Unconstrained mode by pressing Ctrl+S. When operating in Unconstrained mode, the Texture Explorer generates patterns without regard to maintaining a seamlessly-tileable state. This can result in a wider, more unpredictable variety of textures that don't conform to tileable laws. When in Unconstrained mode, adjust the Equalizer controls to enter a new realm of possibilities.

> **NOTE** *The Unconstrained mode works well in combination with the Tile Size of Selection tiling function to create a texture that fills your selection end-to-end. You can return to Constrained mode by pressing Ctrl+S again.* ●

If possible, try spending some time loading presets into the Texture Explorer and observe the settings in the Equalizer. In time you will begin to develop an understanding of how the settings in the Equalizer relate visually to the texture.

Power Texture Creation

NOTE *The Power Texture Creation with the Gradient Designer, like the Equalizer, is a Windows-only feature.* •

A previously mentioned Texture Explorer feature specific to the Windows version of KPT allows users to launch the Gradient Designer extension from within the Texture Explorer by pressing Ctrl+G. This allows you to set up your desktop for "power" texture creation.

To set up your desktop for optimal texture creation with maximum control, follow these steps:

1. Open a new image in RGB mode.

2. Start the KPT Texture Explorer extension. If desired, start the Texture Explorer with the spacebar depressed to bring the user interface up against a black background.

3. Type Ctrl+E to launch the Equalizer.

4. Type Ctrl+G to launch the Gradient Designer.

5. In the Gradient Designer, double-click on the KAI icon to shrink the window size.

6. Click-and-drag the user interfaces to reposition them in a way where you can access them separately (see fig. 5.13).

With this arrangement you now can access all of the Texture Explorer, Equalizer, and related gradient functions simultaneously. Any changes made in the Gradient Designer or Equalizer will be immediately updated in the Current Texture Preview window. Any new presets or changes made in the Texture Explorer will update the Equalizer and Gradient Designer with the new information. This arrangement gives you maximum control in the texture creation process.

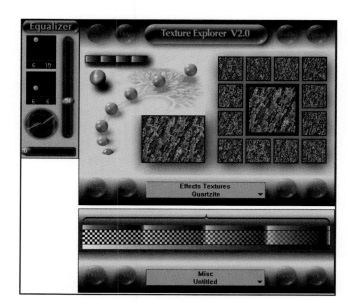

FIGURE 5.13

Power texture creation with the Gradient Designer under Windows.

Under Windows, the KPT user interfaces, especially the Texture Explorer, consume a significant amount of your system resources. It might be necessary to shut-down any nonessential applications, except your paint program or plug-in compatible application, for all of KPT's functions to work properly. If you are not able to access certain functions or menus, try shutting down applications not related to your KPT work ●

Creating Compound Textures

Using the Texture Explorer you can create "compound" textures, or textures composed of multiple applications of single textures. Compound textures take advantage of KPT's apply modes by layering two or more single textures into a composite. Compound textures can be made to look like complex three-dimensional surfaces, painterly color washes, or even liquid-like metals. The following three groups of mini-tutorials show you how the creation of compound textures are accomplished.

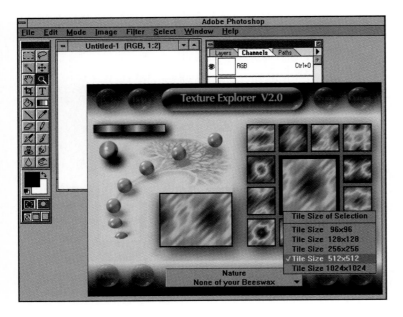

FIGURE 5.14

Open a new RGB image, start the Texture Explorer, load the preset Nature/None of your Beeswax, *set tiling size to Size of Selection, set apply mode to Normal Apply, and click on OK.*

FIGURE 5.15

Restart the Texture Explorer, load the preset Fire/Gray Flaymes, *set tiling to Size of Selection, set apply mode to Multiply Apply, and click on OK.*

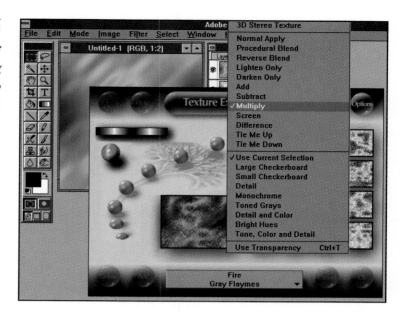

FIGURE 5.16

Restart the Texture Explorer, load the preset Metals/Sensuous, *set tiling size to Size of Selection, set apply mode to Multiply Apply, and click on OK.*

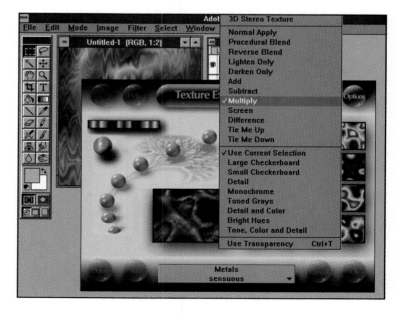

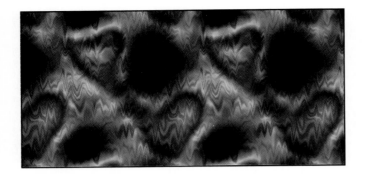

Figure 5.17

The final compound tileable texture filled into a larger image.

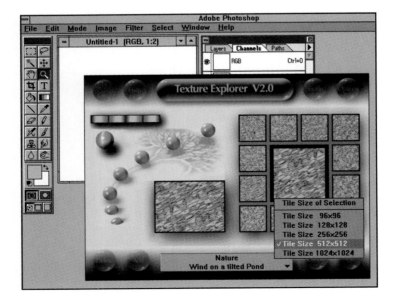

Figure 5.18

Open a new RGB image, start the Texture Explorer, load the preset Nature/Wood on a tilted Pond, *set tiling to Size of Selection, set apply mode to Normal Apply, and click on OK.*

FIGURE **5.19**

Restart the Texture Explorer, load the preset Metals/Pillowy Copper, *set tiling to Size of Selection, set apply mode to Subtract Apply, and click on OK.*

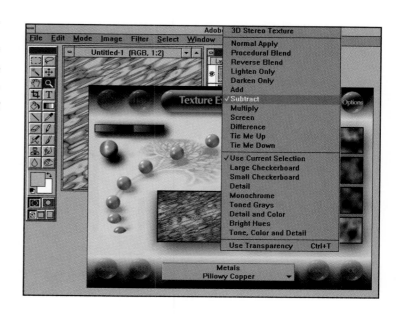

FIGURE **5.20**

Restart the Texture Explorer, load the preset Fire/Diffracted Inferno, *set tiling to Size of Selection, set apply mode to Procedural Blend Apply, and click on OK.*

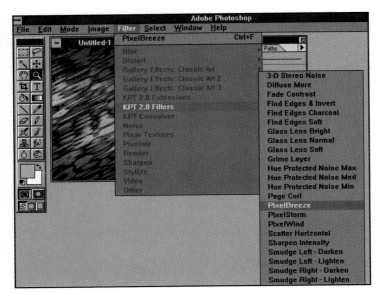

FIGURE 5.21

Apply the PixelBreeze filter with the 2 key depressed (intensity of 2).

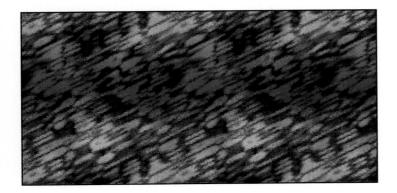

FIGURE 5.22

The final compound tileable texture filled into a larger image.

FIGURE 5.23

Open a new RGB image, start the Texture Explorer, load the preset Wood/Frax, set tiling to Size of Selection, set apply mode to Normal Apply, and click on OK.

FIGURE 5.24

Restart the Texture Explorer, load the preset Liquids/Smooth ooze, set tiling to Size of Selection, set apply mode to Procedural Blend Apply, and click on OK.

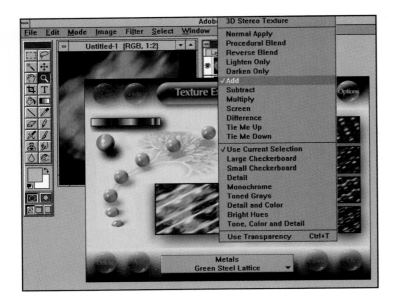

Figure 5.25
Restart the Texture Explorer, load the preset Metals/Green Steel Lattice, *set tiling to Size of Selection, set apply mode to Add Apply, and click on OK.*

FIGURE 5.26
The final compound tileable texture filled into a larger image.

Using the Texture Explorer's Textures in 3D Rendering Software

The Texture Explorer's texture output is ideally suited for the creation of 3D materials used in 3D rendering software programs. The Texture Explorer's tileable properties, in combination with its ability to generate textures at any resolution, makes the Texture Explorer a powerful companion to 3D rendering programs. The following group of images provides a visual demonstration of how KPT's textures can be utilized in several 3D materials. Most of them rely on a combination of a Texture Explorer texture in color, accompanied by a grayscale version of the same texture used as a bump, illumination, or opacity map.

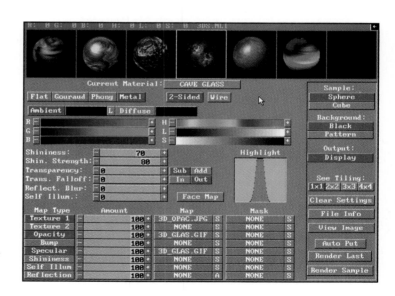

FIGURE 5.27

The 3D Studio Materials Editor with KPT textures.

Texture Map
Diffuse Color RGB 164, 149, 48

Refelection Map
Grayscale w/HP Noise added

3D Rendered Object w/material applied

FIGURE 5.28

Using a Texture Explorer texture as a reflection map in combination with a diffuse color.

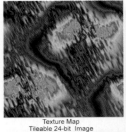

Texture Map
Tileable 24-bit Image

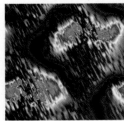

Bump Map (at 100%)
Grayscale Version of Texture Map

3D Rendered Object w/material applied

FIGURE 5.29

Using a Texture Explorer texture as a color map and again in grayscale as a bump map (extreme intensity).

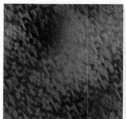

Texture Map
Tileable 24-bit Image

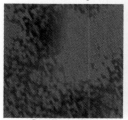

Bump Map (at 15%)
Grayscale Version of Texture Map

3D Rendered Object w/material applied

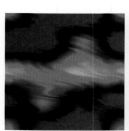

Texture Map
Tileable 24-bit Image

FIGURE 5.31

Using a Texture Explorer texture as a color map and again in grayscale as a self-illumination map.

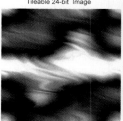

Illumination Map
Grayscale Version of Texture Map

3D Rendered Object w/material applied

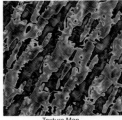

Texture Map
Tileable 24-bit Image

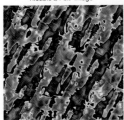

Opacity and Specular Map
Grayscale Version of Texture Map

3D Rendered Object w/material applied

FIGURE 5.32

Using a Texture Explorer texture as a color map and again in grayscale as an opacity (transparency and a specular (highlight) map.

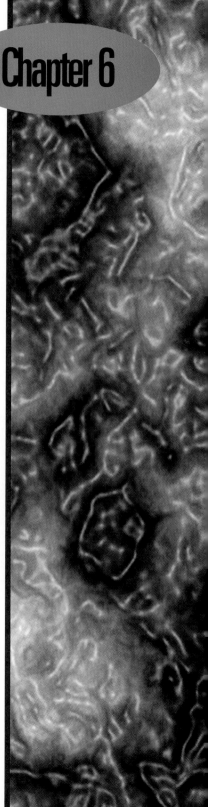

Chapter 6

The Fractal Explorer

$\mathscr{A}$lthough the history of fractals can be traced back as far as the late 19th century, the concept really achieved coherence with the work of mathematician Benoit Mandelbrot. Mandelbrot started working for IBM in 1958 mathematically analyzing electronic noise. During this time, he observed structures within the noise that iterated in a self-repeating hierarchy. Piecing together fragments of earlier mathematicians' research with his own, Mandelbrot's work evolved into the science of fractals as we know it. His papers, books, and lectures in combination with rapidly advancing computer technology made visualization of fractals possible on computers.

Fractals on personal computers initially came about after the introduction of the IBM PC in the early 1980s. A major pioneer in making fractals accessible to non-programmers and artists was the Stone Soup Group, a collaboration of programmers who gather in CompuServe's Graphics Developers forum (an online electronic forum for graphics programmers). The Stone Soup group developed a freeware program called Fractint, a PC-based software package that generates an enormous variety of fractal types and displays them on the computer screen. In its 19th revision, Fractint is considered the father of PC fractal programs; versions can be found for PC, Mac, and Unix platforms.

Put simply, fractals are mathematical algorithms that generate mathematical "objects" or a set of points that represent a pattern. The most frequently seen fractal is the Mandelbrot set. Its shape consists of several adjoining circular areas outlined by an intricate detailed border. This border, when magnified, reveals a complex series of recursive shapes. Steadily increasing the magnification gives way to new patterns embedded within. These patterns tend to resemble patterns found in the natural world. Things like leaves, seashells, snowflakes, and coastlines are a few of the natural shapes imitated by fractals. The Julia set, named after mathematician Gaston Julia, is an iteration of the Mandelbrot set with more complex and interesting variations. Fortunately, the Fractal Explorer enables us to explore the graphical beauty of fractals without having to understand the complex math behind them.

KPT's Fractal Explorer extension brings several varieties of the popular Mandelbrot and Julia type fractals to the KPT toolkit, along with a few hybrid versions. Unlike other fractal generators, the Fractal Explorer generates fractals in 24-bit color, and gives you complete control of colors and transparency in the interior and exterior of the fractal using gradients from the Gradient Designer. All of KPT's apply modes are in the Fractal Explorer, enabling you to blend fractals in many ways with underlying imagery. Like the other KPT extensions, the Fractal Explorer comes with a collection of presets, and you can save your discoveries as new presets.

Unraveling the Interface

The Fractal Explorer interface is made of several different controls and windows that enable you to create fractal designs (see fig. 6.1). The following section provides information about the functions of each of these elements.

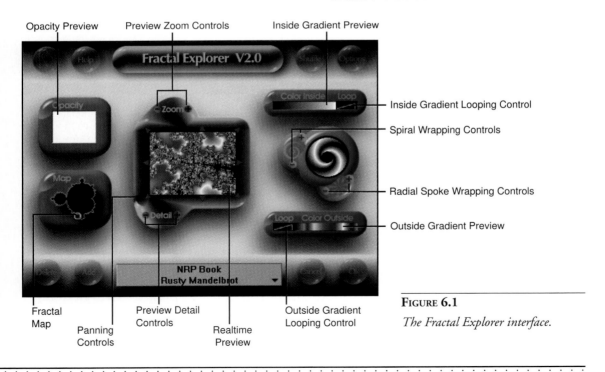

Opacity Preview Preview Zoom Controls Inside Gradient Preview

Inside Gradient Looping Control

Spiral Wrapping Controls

Radial Spoke Wrapping Controls

Outside Gradient Preview

Fractal Map Preview Detail Controls Outside Gradient Looping Control
Panning Controls Realtime Preview

FIGURE 6.1

The Fractal Explorer interface.

The Realtime Preview Window

In the center of the Fractal Explorer interface is the familiar Realtime Preview window (see fig. 6.2). This window displays the current fractal image, and functions as your window while navigating fractal space.

Zooming and Panning Controls

The "current" fractal in the Realtime Preview window is actually a small section of the entire mathematical construct. Imagine yourself floating over the fractal plane, looking down at it through a telescope. As you move at a constant altitude over the plane, you are "panning" the view in the telescope. Increasing the magnification of the telescope increases the zoom factor, allowing you to view more detail but constraining your field of view to a smaller region of the plane. Conversely, decreasing the zoom factor decreases the magnification, resulting in a larger region view but less detail. These controls have been integrated into the Realtime Preview window's functionality.

Zooming and panning are the main tools for exploring fractals in the Fractal Explorer. These are the tools that enable you to navigate and examine the Fractal Map, a rectangular area that contains the fractal patterns. The panning tools let you scroll from one area of the map to another. The zooming tools let you magnify a specific area, or pull back from the map to see a larger area.

Zooming In and Out

Zooming is the process of getting closer or farther from the fractal map, similar to increasing or decreasing the magnification of a telescope. Zoom all the way out to see the entire fractal map, or zoom in tight to see extreme detail. The Fractal Explorer's Undo command ($\mathcal{H}$+Z for the Mac or Ctrl+Z for Windows) undoes one level of Zoom command.

You can zoom by using two methods. For direct zooming, move the cursor over the Realtime

FIGURE 6.2

The Realtime Preview/current fractal window.

Preview window. The cursor changes into a magnifying glass (see fig. 6.3). Click to zoom in one level at a time. To zoom out one level at a time, hold down the Options key (Mac) or Alt key (Windows) while the cursor is over the Realtime Preview window and click. Each time you perform a zoom, the display in the Realtime Preview window is updated, centering on the point where you clicked. This updating rerenders the fractal in the Realtime Preview window and requires three passes to complete. You can, however, click to zoom another level at anytime before the redraw process is complete.

Another zooming method, known as *centered zooming*, is available through the controls built into the upper-left part of the frame surrounding the Realtime Preview window. On either side of the word Zoom are the + and - symbols (see fig. 6.4). Click on + to zoom in or - to zoom out one level at a time. Unlike the direct zooming commands, centered zooming keeps the view centered on the same point in the Realtime Preview window.

Clicking and holding on the word Zoom brings up the zoom slider bar (see fig. 6.5). This enables you to zoom on a very large scale by dragging the slider to increase or decrease the percentage of

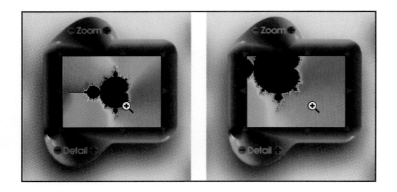

FIGURE 6.3
The cursor changes to a magnifying glass when you direct zoom.

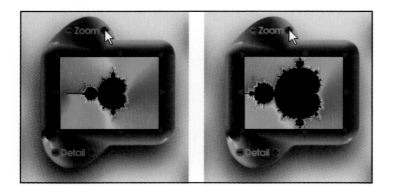

FIGURE 6.4
The + and - symbols used for centered zooming.

zoom. Each time you change the slider position, the percentage scale is reset making the current zoom level 100 percent. This makes it somewhat difficult to return precisely to a previous zoom level.

NOTE *The value to the left of the percentage in the Detail Slider bar is the Zoom Radius value. Check the Zoom Radius value setting in the Numerical Input dialog, accessible under the Fractal Explorer's Options menu. This stores the actual value for the current Zoom level. Note the Zoom Radius value, then return to the same Zoom level at a later time by retyping the value in the dialog box. The value is saved with a fractal preset as well. See the "Numerical Input Options" section later in this chapter for more information.* •

Remember that ⌘+Z (Mac) or Ctrl+Z (Windows) will undo one level of zooming.

Panning and Navigating the Fractal Map

The fractal map, located to the lower left of the Realtime Preview window (see fig. 6.6), is a control that displays an image of the classic Mandelbrot set. This control serves two functions. The first enables you to pick the type of Mandelbrot or Julia set to use, and the second enables you to circle the location on the fractal map to explore.

To pick a fractal map type, click and hold in the fractal map to reveal a small menu of choices. Drag and release on the fractal map type of your choice. The selections available to you include the Mandelbrot set, Julia sets I, II, and III, and two new Mandelbrot-Julia hybrids.

Inside the fractal map is a small red circle that indicates the area on the map that represents the center of the view shown in the Realtime Preview window. Hold down the ⌘ key (Mac) or Ctrl key

FIGURE 6.5

The zoom slider bar.

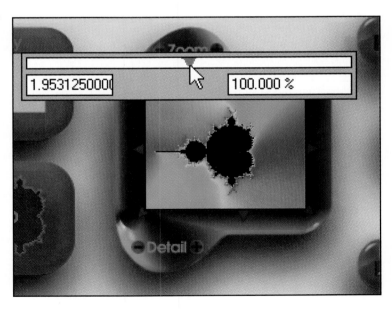

Figure 6.6

Navigating the fractal map.

(Windows), then click-and-drag the red circle to a new area on the fractal map to explore a different area of the map. Keep in mind that this red circle signifies the center of the view in the Realtime Preview window, but is not related in any way to the zoom factor. Moving the red circle around enables you to travel to any region of the fractal map quickly.

For finer movement, there is a set of small arrows bordering the Realtime Preview window (see fig. 6.7). Click on one to pan the view in the direction of the arrow. This control enables you to pan in any direction, moving within a smaller region of the fractal map.

Lastly, you can pan the view by holding down the ⌘ key (Mac) or Ctrl key (Windows), then clicking and dragging in the Realtime Preview window (see fig. 6.8). This feature gives you the finest level of control when trying to position the view. Use

this control when you want to position the view precisely inside the Realtime Preview window.

Setting the Amount of Fractal Detail

By now you might have discovered that as you zoom closer to the fractal, more detail and new patterns are revealed. Increasing the Detail settings increases the amount of detail that appears within the given zoom level.

The Detail Settings control can be found in the lower right region of the frame surrounding the Realtime Preview window (see fig. 6.9). Similar in functionality to the Zoom controls, the Detail Settings increase or decrease the amount of detail for the given fractal. Clicking on the + or - symbols increases or decreases the amount of detail.

Clicking and holding on the word Detail brings up a slider bar (see fig. 6.10) that enables you to change the Detail Settings on a larger scale, similar

FIGURE 6.7

Panning with the arrow controls.

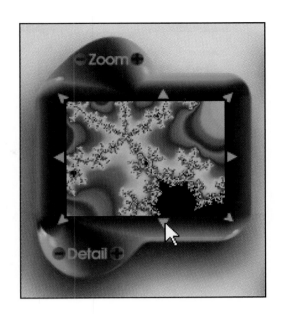

FIGURE 6.8

Direct panning by dragging.

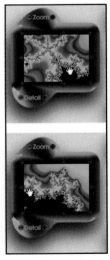

in functionality to the Zoom control's slider bar. Each time you change the slider position, the percentage scale is reset to make the current level 100 percent. This makes it somewhat difficult to return precisely to a previous Detail level.

NOTE *The value to the left of the percentage in the Detail Slider bar is the Stop Iterate value (see fig. 6.10). Check the Stop Iterate value setting in the Numerical Input dialog, accessible under the Fractal Explorer's Options menu. This is where the value for the current Detail level is stored. Note the Stop Iterate value, then return to the same Detail level at a later time by re-typing the value into the dialog box. The value is saved with a fractal preset as well. See the section "Numerical Input Options" later in this chapter for more information.* •

Remember that ⌘+Z (Mac) or Ctrl+Z (Windows) will undo one level of Detail changes.

The tradeoff to increasing the level of detail is an increase in the amount of time necessary to render the fractal. In fractal terminology, increasing the level of detail is known as increasing the number of iterations. A higher number of iterations increases the computational time required to produce the additional detail.

Numerical Input Options

The Numerical Input option, accessible from the Options menu, opens a dialog box containing several input boxes for numerical entry (see fig. 6.11). This dialog box enables those experienced with fractal formulas to enter their own variables for generating new iterations. The Numerical Input dialog box also displays the settings of the current fractal. This information is saved with the presets so that you can use them as a starting point for exploring the different parameters in the dialog box.

The Mandelbrot set is basically a graph. On the X axis are real numbers, and on the Y axis are imaginary numbers. The first four boxes in the Fractal Explorer numerical input dialog box, labeled as Z Real, Z Imag, C Real, and C Image, are the X and

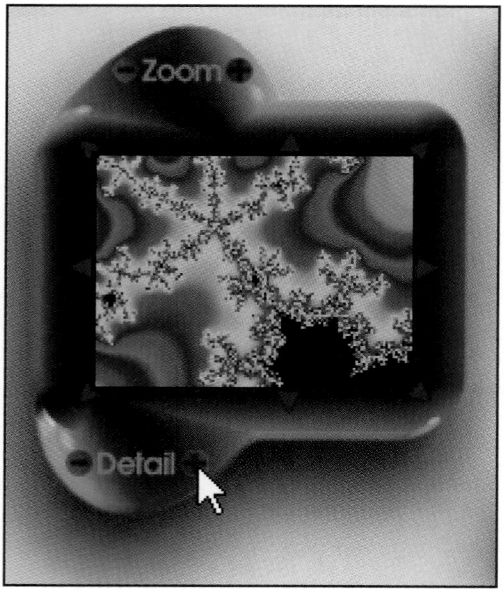

FIGURE 6.9

Use the Detail Settings to set the amount of detail.

FIGURE 6.10

The Detail slider control.

FIGURE 6.11

The Numerical Entry dialog box.

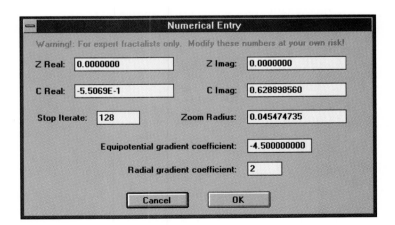

Y coordinates of two points, Z and C. These coordinates are expressed as complex numbers in the form of X-coordinate + (square-root of -1) × Y-coordinate.

Underneath the C and Z entry boxes in the Numerical Input dialog box are the following four boxes:

◆ The Stop Iterate box contains the value for the current fractal's Detail setting. The Stop Iterate value is an integer between 32 and 16,384.

◆ The Zoom Radius box contains the value for the current fractal's Zoom factor. The Zoom Radius value is a number ranging between 3.4E-18 to 8.

◆ The Equipotential gradient coefficient box contains the value for the current fractal's Spiral Control setting. The Equipotential Coefficient value is a number between -200 and 200. See the section "The Gradient Wrapping Controls" later in this chapter for more information about the Spiral control.

◆ The Radial gradient coefficient box contains the value for the current fractal's Spoke setting. The Radial gradient coefficient value is an integer between -200 and 200. See the section "The Gradient Wrapping Controls" later in this chapter for more information about the Radial control.

Controlling the Colors

The preceding sections of this chapter discuss controlling the pattern characteristics of a fractal. The following section provides information about controlling the color attributes of fractals.

Color Inside and Color Outside Controls

Two similar controls are to the right of the Realtime Preview window (see fig. 6.12). They are called the Color Inside and Color Outside controls. They provide access to the Gradient Designer's presets and looping controls, and enable you to use a preset gradient as color information for the current fractal. They also display the current gradient and looping type in a small preview mode right on the front of the control.

In the Fractal Explorer, you can color both the interior (inside) and the exterior (outside) of the fractal set. To see this relationship, load the preset *Black Interior/White Exterior* from the NRP Book category. Note the relationship between the interior and exterior of the fractal set. The interior area, colored black, is like a lake surrounded by white shoreline.

The Color Outside menu control supplies the gradient colors and transparency information for the exterior of the fractal set (see fig. 6.13), where users most frequently apply color. On the right side of the control is the Gradient Preview window, which displays the gradient colors currently in use in the fractal. This window also acts as a button for choosing a preset gradient. Notice that as you pass the mouse pointer over the control, a pointer/page icon appears. Just click-and-hold on the Gradient Preview window to activate a menu similar to the Presets menu in the Gradient Designer. Drag and release on a new preset, and the Gradient

FIGURE 6.12

The color controls.

FIGURE 6.13

Accessing exterior gradients presets.

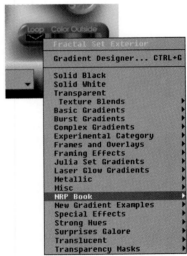

Preview window displays the new gradient while the Realtime Preview window fractal display is updated with the new colors. On the left side of the control is the gradient's looping setting, which also acts as a button enabling you to change the looping type. Click-and-hold on the gradient looping preview to activate a menu with other looping options.

NOTE *The gradient presets can be cycled by using the left arrow and right arrow keys to move up or down through the presets one at a time.* •

The Color Inside control supplies the gradient color and transparency information for the interior of the fractal set (see fig. 6.14). Coloring this space opens up some interesting possibilities for color blends that interact with the exterior colors. The Color Inside control's functionality is identical to that of the Color Outside control. Its operation is identical as well, with the exception that you cannot cycle the presets in the Color Inside gradient preview window using the keyboard direction keys (left arrow and right arrow). The interior gradient presets can only be changed with the drop-down Preset menu.

The Gradient Wrapping Controls

Beyond choosing and applying colors to your gradient set, an additional control known as the Gradient Wrapping control (located between the Gradient Preview Bars) provides unique looping capabilities (refer back to fig. 6.1).

On the upper left part of the Gradient Wrapping control frame there is a control known as the Spiral Wrapping control. It controls how rapidly the colors in the gradient change as they wrap around the exterior of the fractal, and how densely the gradient colors are packed together. This has the effect of increasing or decreasing the amount of detail by adding or subtracting more of the gradient's colors from the mix. Just click on the + or - symbols to increase or decrease the color cycling rate. Reset the control to zero by clicking once on the spiral symbol between the + and - symbols.

The small circular preview window in the center of the Gradient Wrapping control (see fig. 6.15)

provides a visual reference to the degree of spiral setting with a series of concentric rings. The higher the spiral setting, the more circular rings appear in the preview window.

On the lower right part of the Gradient Wrapping control frame is a control known as the Radial Spoke Wrapping control (see fig. 6.16). It controls how often the entire gradient pattern is repeated in a 360 degree circle around exterior of the fractal set. Increase or decrease the Spoke setting by clicking on the + or - symbol. Reset the control to zero by clicking on the spoke symbol between the + and - symbols.

Like radio or water waves, the Spiral and Spoke controls generate wave-like patterns that intersect, creating interesting patterns at nodal lines and other points. You can manipulate both settings simultaneously by clicking and dragging in the Gradient Wrapping control's preview window. Dragging in a left or right direction affects the Spiral settings, and dragging up or down affects the Spoke settings. This provides a quicker alternative to using the controls separately.

HSC warns that setting the Spoke control to anything other then 0 might introduce small artifacts or irregularities in the fractal image. These sometimes show up as scattered pixels in the exterior fractal area that have the same colors as pixels in the fractal's interior area. These might be specific to a certain area of the fractal map; try moving to a different area to eliminate them.

FIGURE **6.14**

Accessing interior gradient presets.

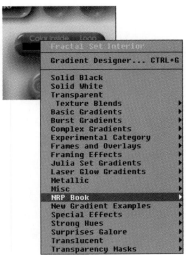

FIGURE **6.15**

Adjusting the Spiral setting.

NOTE *Using your paint program, you can easily retouch small artifacts. Try a cloning tool like Photoshop's Rubber Stamp to grab a nearby group of pixels and copy it over an artifact.* ●

The Apply Modes and Opacity Selector

The apply modes found in the other KPT extensions are also found in the Fractal Explorer (see fig. 6.17). They can be accessed by choosing the Options menu.

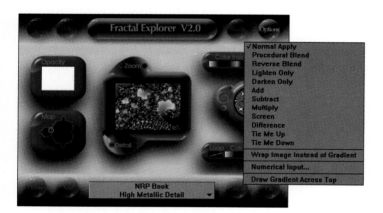

FIGURE **6.16**

Adjusting the Spoke setting.

FIGURE **6.17**

The apply modes menu.

The Realtime Preview window displays the current fractal and its interaction with the underlying image whenever a non-normal apply mode is selected, or if the gradient contains transparency elements. The Fractal Explorer enables you to preview this interaction against a selection of test patterns and images, just like in the other KPT extensions. Instead of accessing these settings from the Options menu, however, the Fractal Explorer

contains an enhanced control known as the Opacity Selector.

The Opacity Selector can be found directly above the Fractal Map control, and contains a window that displays the current Test Image. This window also serves as a button. Click and hold on it to select which Test Image you want to use. The choices include the current underlying image, the system clipboard, or the seven stock images in the

KPT suite (see fig. 6.18). The stock images are a small collection of images that represent a wide range of color and grayscale imagery. By previewing against a few of the stock images, you can gain a feel for how your design will respond to different underlying imagery. For more information on the test images, see Chapter 2, "Unraveling the Interface."

The Opacity Selector helps when you are working with a detailed or complex fractal that includes many transparent areas. It also serves as a reference point when testing different apply modes on the current fractal.

Wrap Image Instead of Gradient

Another color manipulation option is the Wrap Image Instead of Gradient option. This can be enabled by selecting it from the Fractal Explorer's Options menu. This feature reads the underlying selection, image, or system clipboard and grabs the colors for use in the current fractal. Similar and more direct than the Gradient Designer's Load Gradient from Image option, the Wrap Image option is a great way to match the colors in your fractal with the existing colors in your image.

A neat trick is to start with a color image, then start the Texture Explorer using the Wrap Image option. Now utilize an Apply mode such as Procedural Blend to blend the fractal into the underlying selection or image. This blends the fractal patterns in with the image in a subtle and interesting way.

There's no direct method for converting the colors from the Wrap Image option into a gradient. A workaround, however, is to enable the Load Normal Gradient from image option in the Gradient Designer preferences (see fig. 6.19). Then, make a rectangular selection within the image and restart the Gradient Designer. The colors will load into the Gradient Designer, which you then can save as a preset gradient for use in the Fractal Explorer.

Draw Gradient Across Top

The Draw Gradient Across Top option (see fig. 6.20) also is accessed from the Options menu. When enabled, this option renders the actual gradient color strip from the exterior fractal gradient

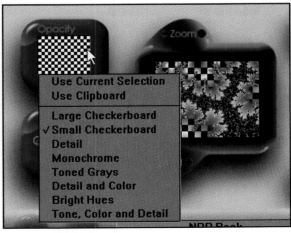

FIGURE 6.18

The Opacity menu.

across the top of the underlying selection or image. By rendering the gradient to the actual bitmap, you can select it and load it as a gradient into the Gradient Designer.

The Draw Gradient Across Top option also allows you to perform color corrections or other changes to the gradient strip while in bitmap form. Select

the area and start the Gradient Designer to load the modified strip as the current gradient.

If the Wrap Image option is enabled, the Draw Gradient Across Top option will render a strip containing only a solid color, usually the plug-in compatible application's foreground palette color. In addition, the Draw Gradient Across Top option is

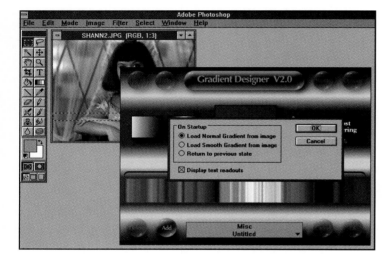

FIGURE 6.19

Loading a gradient from the image.

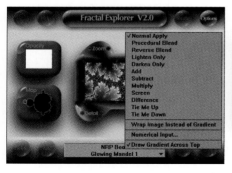

FIGURE 6.20

The Draw Gradient Across Top option.

saved with a preset. Many of the stock Fractal Explorer presets have this option enabled, so be sure to check the status of this option before committing the design to an image.

The Shuffle Button

The Shuffle button works in the same way as its counterpart in the other extensions. Clicking once on the Shuffle button randomly shuffles the Interior Colors, Exterior Colors, Exterior Looping, Interior Looping, Apply Mode, Test Image, Equipotential Speed, and Radial Speed. Use the Shuffle button to explore different attribute options randomly. Clicking and holding on the Shuffle button produces a menu that enables you to control what attributes get shuffled, on an individual or global basis (see fig. 6.21).

FIGURE 6.21

The Shuffle button and Shuffle menu.

The Presets Menu

The Presets menu is located at the bottom center of the Fractal Explorer user interface. It works exactly the same way as the presets in the rest of the KPT suite. The Fractal Explorer comes with over 50 preset fractal designs. They are stored in one category, called Factory Presets (see fig. 6.22). You can save new presets into any existing category or create your own categories.

You also can move through the presets using the keyboard equivalent commands. The up arrow and down arrow keys move between the previous and next presets in a category. The Page Up and Page Down move between the previous and next category, and the Home and End keys move to the first and last category, respectively.

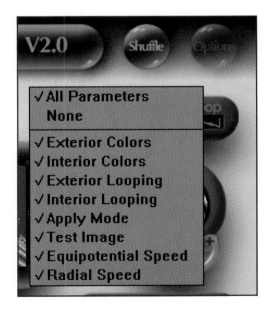

FIGURE **6.22**

The Fractal Explorer presets.

Exploring a Fractal—The Basics

To get a grip on what the Fractal Explorer is about, follow these steps.

1. Open a new document in RGB mode, 320×240 pixels in size.

2. Start the Fractal Explorer extension.

3. Load the preset *And Mandelbrot Said* from the Factor Presets Category.

In this preset, you are zoomed all the way out so that the entire map is visible in the Realtime Preview window. Notice how the red circle in the Fractal Map is near the center of the map, and how the colors for the exterior and interior gradients relate the colors in the Realtime Preview window (see fig. 6.23).

4. Move the mouse over the Realtime Preview window to change the pointer into a magnifying glass.

5. Pick a point to zoom in to in the fractal along the border between the exterior and interior areas.

6. Click five times on that spot to perform a five-level zoom. This will magnify the chosen area centered on the point you click.

You have zoomed in to a specific area of the fractal map. Note how the red circle in the Fractal Map is now centered on the area you picked (see fig. 6.24).

7. Pick a new point within the magnified fractal in the Realtime Preview window, then click on it three times to zoom three more levels.

Try changing the exterior or interior gradient colors, the Gradient Wrapping controls, or the Detail Levels and observe the effects on the current fractal (see fig. 6.25). These functions are the foundation of fractal exploration, and should lead you to some interesting places.

FIGURE 6.23

Loading the preset And Mandelbrot Said.

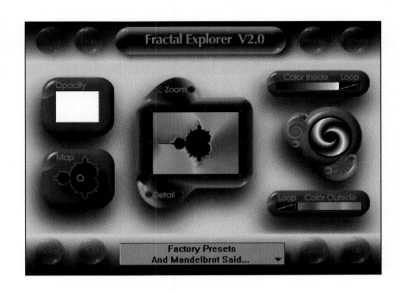

FIGURE 6.24

Zooming five times using direct zoom.

FIGURE **6.25**

Zooming another three times using direct zoom.

Power Fractal Creation—Windows Users Only

To set up your desktop for optimal fractal creation with maximum color control, follow these steps:

1. Open a new image in RGB mode.

2. Start the KPT Fractal Explorer extension. If desired, start the Fractal Explorer with the spacebar depressed to bring the user-interface up against a black background.

3. Press Ctrl+G to launch the Gradient Designer.

4. In the Gradient Designer, double-click on the KAI icon to shrink the window size.

5. Click-and-drag the user interfaces to reposition them so that you can access them all separately.

With this arrangement, you now can access all of the Fractal Explorer and related gradient functions simultaneously. Any changes made in the Gradient Designer are immediately updated in the Realtime Preview window. Any new presets or changes made in the Fractal Explorer will update the Gradient Designer with the new information. This arrangement gives you maximum control in the fractal creation process (see fig. 6.26).

Try the Ctrl+click and drag function on the Gradient Bar. This color cycles the gradient colors in the current fractal. Accordingly, pressing Ctrl+1, Ctrl+2, Ctrl+3, or Ctrl+4 while clicking and dragging in the Gradient Bar enables you to cycle the red, green, blue, or alpha components of the gradient respectively. Press Alt and click-and-drag to compress or expand the gradient for interesting results.

FIGURE **6.26**

Power fractal creation with the
Gradient Designer.

Part **III**

The Filters and Utilities

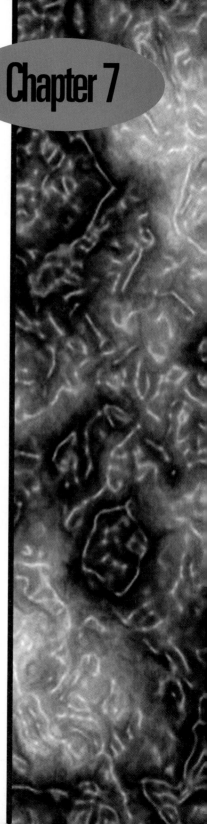

Chapter 7

The Filter Effects

 $\mathcal{A}$ n image-processing filter really is a piece of software code that performs a mathematical operation on a pixel or group of pixels within a digital image. The result of this mathematical operation is a change in the pixel's color characteristics such as hue, saturation, and intensity. Some filters shuffle pixels over a given area, creating a scattering effect on the image. Some filters blur an image, and others sharpen them. Some filters actually are mini-programs that run within a host software application. Regardless of the function of a filter, the concept of filters relies on analyzing existing pixels within an image or selection, then altering them through the application of a mathematical formula. This process also is known as *convolution*.

KPT includes over 25 one-step filters that provide a variety of different effects, with built-in control over intensity and other parameters. You can use the KPT filters to add noise or texture, distort and smudge pixels, warp regions into 3D spheres, or apply subtle diffusion and distortion effects. In the next two chapters, you'll see how these filters work, and their effects on an image at different intensity settings.

The term one-step filter is a bit misleading. Most of the KPT filters do their most effective work when used multiple times at the same or varying intensities. The filter intensities and other settings are retained in memory after application on an image or selection. By pressing ⌘+F (Macintosh) or Ctrl+F (Windows) to repeat the last filter operation, Photoshop users can repeat application of a given filter one or more times with a single key-stroke combination. ●

The Filters—One Step and Beyond

The KPT filters have a variety of different names, but can be classified into six categories. These categories include the Diffusion, Distortion, Noise, Color, Blur, and Utility filters. Although the filters are called one-step, many of them produce great effects when applied repeatedly at the same or varying intensities.

All KPT filters can be found under the plug-in filters section of your plug-in compatible application. In Photoshop for the Macintosh, they can be found under the Filters menu mixed into the filter categories beginning with the name KPT. In Photoshop for Windows, they can be found under the Filters menu in the KPT 2.0 Filters section. The KPT filters must be installed into your plug-in folder or directory for them to appear in the Filters menu. For the filters to work, you first must open a truecolor or grayscale image to provide the filters with pixels to operate on.

Most of the filters work in combination with the keyboard. The number keys (1 through 0) control either intensity, direction, or other attributes depending on which filter you are using. The Caps Lock key provides alternate capabilities on some filters as well. You must hold down one of these keys while executing a given filter. This action enables you to control various parameters on a scale of 1 to 10 (keys 1 to 0, with keys 2 to 9 as intermediate increments), and some special case alternates (Caps Lock). The default setting typically is 5, or 50 percent intensity.

The Diffusion Filters

The Diffusion group of filters analyze a given pixel, then shuffle the surrounding pixels over a finite area to create a diffused effect. This effect can make an image or selection appear to have fine painterly qualities, or appear as if viewed through frosted glass, or even diffuse an image beyond recognition into a mass of colors. KPT's diffusion filters include Diffuse More, Pixel Breeze, Pixel Wind, Pixel Storm, and Scatter Horizontal.

Diffuse More

The Diffuse More filter shuffles the pixels within an image over an area described by HSC as being "about 4 times the cell size" of Photoshop's normal Diffuse filter (see fig. 7.1). The intensity of the effect is controlled through the numeric keys 1 through 0. Hold down 1 while executing Diffuse More for the least intensity; hold down 0 for the highest intensity.

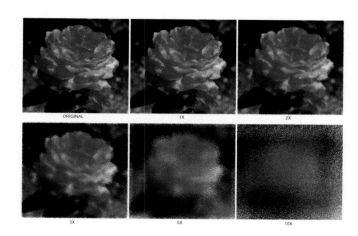

The Diffuse More filter is useful for softening or fuzzying a given area, giving it a slight painterly look. Use it on scanned photographs and computer-rendered images to remove some of the stark realism or to hide small artifacts.

PixelBreeze

The PixelBreeze filter diffuses or shuffles the pixels in an image over an area 30 pixels in size, while transferring itself in Lighten Apply mode (see fig. 7.2). This is a more subtle diffusion than Diffuse More, and lightens or fades the image when repeated. The intensity of this effect can be controlled through the numeric keys 1 through 0. Hold down 1 while executing PixelBreeze for the least intensity; hold down 0 for the greatest intensity.

The Caps Lock key enables a variation on PixelBreeze (also available in PixelStorm) that works in combination with feathered selections. When executed with Caps Lock depressed, the PixelBreeze filter blurs and blends the effect at the feathered edges with the underlying image. This provides a subtle blending effect that is most noticeable with color images.

Use PixelBreeze to create a subtle softening or dithering effect. At greater intensities, PixelBreeze creates a frosted glass-like distortion effect.

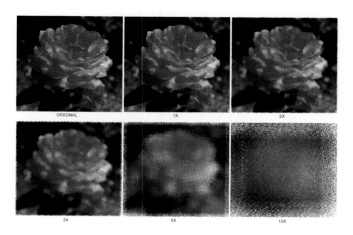

FIGURE 7.2

The PixelBreeze filter applied to an image at 1, 2, 3, 5, and 10 intensity.

PixelWind

The PixelWind filter diffuses the pixels in an image over an area approximately 80 pixels in size, while using a Darken Apply mode (see fig. 7.3). It uses a slightly different algorithm than the PixelStorm or PixelBreeze filters, and yields a different effect. The intensity of this effect can be controlled through the numeric keys 1 through 0. Hold down 1 while executing PixelWind for the least intensity; hold down 0 for the greatest intensity. The Caps Lock key has no effect in this filter.

PixelWind has the effect of darkening and increasing the saturation of the image while diffusing the pixels. Repeated applications of this filter can send your image into the depths of darkness and extreme color. A single application at high intensity (8-9) can produce an effect resembling grainy overexposed photographs.

PixelStorm

PixelStorm takes diffusion to the extreme, shuffling the pixels of an image over a 200 pixel-wide area while using a Darken Apply mode. The intensity of this effect can be controlled through the numeric keys 1 through 0. Hold down 1 while executing PixelBreeze for the least intensity, hold down 0 for the greatest intensity. When executed with Caps Lock depressed, the PixelStorm filter blurs and blends the effect at the feathered edges with the underlying image. This provides a subtle blending effect that is most noticeable with color images.

When applied with an intensity of 1, PixelStorm produces a subtle and beautiful diffusion effect, softening an image. At high intensity, PixelStorm diffuses the image into oblivion, resulting in a dark mass of color (see fig. 7.4). Repeated application can remove all detail and edging from an image.

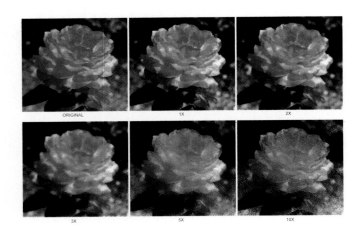

FIGURE 7.3

The PixelWind filter applied to an image at 1, 2, 3, 5, and 10 intensity.

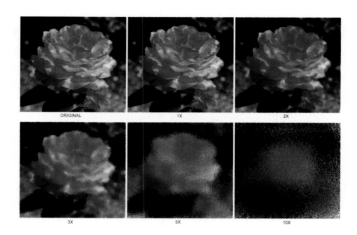

FIGURE 7.4

The PixelStorm filter applied to an image at 1, 2, 3, 5, and 10 intensity.

Scatter Horizontal

The Scatter Horizontal filter diffuses an image on the horizontal axis while using a Lighten Apply mode (see fig. 7.5). This has the effect of scattering the pixels left and right. The intensity of this effect can be controlled through the numeric keys 1 through 0. Hold down 1 while executing Scatter Horizontal for the least intensity; hold down 0 for the greatest intensity.

This effect can produce some interesting patterns when used on individual RGB channels or with repeated applications. Try applying the effect a few times, invert the image, then rotate the image 45 degrees or 90 degrees and repeat the effect again in one of the RGB channels. A type of digital weave pattern can be created that simulates cloth, or makes a good grayscale displacement map for Photoshop's Displace filter.

FIGURE 7.5

The Scatter Horizontal filter applied to an image at 1, 2, 3, 5, and 10 intensity.

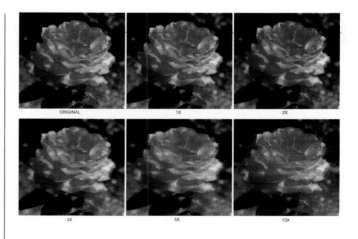

Distortion Filters

The KPT Distortion group of filters include the Glass Lens series and the Vortex Tiling filter. These filters warp a given group of pixels, creating the appearance of 3D rendered objects, or swirling the pixels into twisted patterns.

The Glass Lens Series

Spheres hold a certain fascination for many people because of their simple, perfect beauty and their interaction with light. The KPT Glass Lens filters warp an image in a manner similar to inflating a beach ball underneath the image on a sunny day. The Glass Lens filters actually use a mini-raytracer optimized for creating spherical distortions that resemble shiny balls (see fig. 7.6). This filter works on a selection to isolate a spherical area and distort it outward, rendering an anti-aliased sphere with a specular highlight that simulates the effects of a light source shining on it (complete with shadow).

There are three Glass Lens filters:

♦ **GLASS LENS BRIGHT.** The Glass Lens Bright filter simulates a brightly-lit sphere, with dark shadows and low ambient light.

♦ **GLASS LENS NORMAL.** The Glass Lens Normal filter creates a sphere with a highlight that's about 2/3 the intensity of the Bright filter.

♦ **GLASS LENS SOFT.** The Glass Lens Soft filter produces a much more subtle highlight, with softer less-noticeable shadows on the sphere.

You can simulate light shining onto the sphere from different angles by utilizing the numeric keys 1 through 9. Holding down the 1 key while executing the Glass Lens filters produces a highlight on the lower left of the sphere (similar to the key's position on the numeric keypad, or around 7:30 on a watch). Holding down the 9 key while executing the Glass Lens filter produces a highlight on the upper right of the sphere. The 2, 4, 8, and 6 keys produce highlights on the bottom, left, top, and right sides respectively. The 5 key renders the highlight in the center of the sphere, as if a light was shining from the same location as your eye.

Depressing the Caps Lock key enables a feature useful for rectangular or otherwise non-spherical selections. Holding down the Caps Lock key while executing the Glass Lens filters fills the background behind the sphere with black. This helps to isolate the sphere when rendered against a busy background.

NOTE *For Windows users only, depressing the Scroll Lock key simulates eclipses or negative light situations. Holding down the Scroll Lock key while depressing the 1 key and executing the Glass Lens filters renders a sphere with the eclipse highlight on the far lower left with very dark shadows on the rest of the sphere. Holding down the Scroll Lock key while depressing the 5 key and executing the Glass Lens filters renders a total eclipse with a light outline around the sphere.*

To further challenge your keyboard gymnastic ability, try holding down the following keys while executing the Glass Lens filters:

- *The Scroll Lock key*

- *The Caps Lock key*

- *The 1 key*

The result is a sphere against a black background, an eclipse highlight on the far lower left, and very dark shadows on the sphere. •

Fun with Spheres

Try combinations of Glass Lens Normal and Glass Lens Soft to simulate multiple light sources of different direction and intensities (see fig. 7.7). These effects were created using multiple applications of the Glass Lens filter using different light source directions with each pass.

Try rendering Glass Lens filters on multiple feathered or unusually-shaped selections (see fig. 7.8). These effects were created by first drawing a feathered selection, then applying the Glass Lens filter.

Blend in textures from the Texture Explorer or gradients from the Gradient Designer to texturize your spheres (see fig. 7.10). This effect starts with a selection where Glass Lens has been applied, and then a texture is blended using the KPT Texture Explorer and the Procedural Blend Apply mode.

FIGURE 7.6

The Glass Lens filters applied to an image at various intensities and with various options enabled.

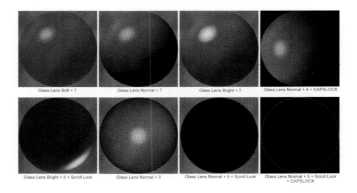

FIGURE 7.7

Multiple light source emulation with the Glass Lens filter.

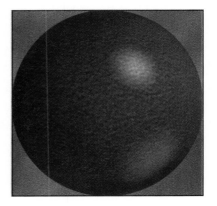

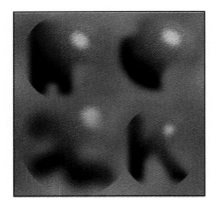

FIGURE 7.8

Using Glass Lens on non-rectangular feathered selections.

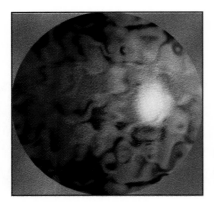

FIGURE 7.9

Using the Glass Lens filter with the Texture Explorer. Use the Procedural Blend Apply mode to blend a texture into the sphere.

Create spherical and ellipsoidal buttons and controls for interfaces (see fig. 7.10). These buttons were created by first rendering the Glass Lens filter to a spherical or elliptical selection, then adding text.

Vortex Tiling

The Vortex Tiling literally turns an image inside out, distorting the image by stretching and warping it around a circular area (see fig. 7.11). This warping can repeat recursively into the center of the image creating the illusion of a long kaleidoscopic tunnel or funnel. The intensity of the vortex effect is controlled by holding down a numeric key (1 through 0) while executing the filter.

FIGURE 7.10

Interface buttons created with the Glass Lens filter. Start with a circular or elliptical selection, apply Glass Lens filter, and overlay distorted or stretched text with a little opacity.

FIGURE 7.11

The Vortex Tiling filter applied to an image at 1, 2, 3, 5, and 10 intensity.

High levels of intensity produce vortexes with many symmetrical, sometimes fractal-like repetitions within the vortex. Repeated applications of the Vortex Tile filter at different intensities can produce unusual effects, sometimes straightening out the pattern into a tile pattern with blurred edges.

Noise Filters

The Noise filters in the KPT filters collection provide a rich set of noise generating tools, useful for adding texture or detail to an image, or for generating completely new images from just noise. The KPT Noise filters include the Grime Layer, Hue Protected Noise, and Special Noise filters.

Grime Layer

The Grime Layer filter generates a special grayscale noise with transparent attributes (see fig. 7.12). This noise overlays onto an image creating effects ranging from haze and fog to dirt. The intensity of this effect can be controlled through the numeric keys 1 through 0. Hold down 1 while executing Grime Layer for the least intensity; hold down 0 for the greatest intensity. Two extra levels of intensity beyond 0 are available by pressing the - or = keys. These extra keys have the effect of adjusting the brightness and contrast levels to their extremes, producing an intense snow effect.

Low-intensity applications of the Grime Layer filter create a subtle grainy haze over an image. Multiple passes at medium to high intensity on a white background create a nice looking starfield. Apply Grime Layer to feathered selections for smokey-like clouds. Layering different sized feathered selections can create the illusion of density in the smoke cloud, rendering a more three-dimensional effect.

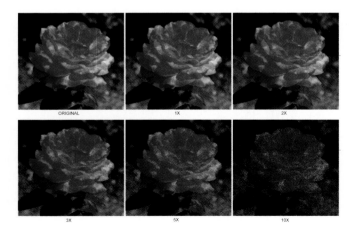

Hue Protected Noise

The Hue Protected Noise filters are a unique set of noise generating filters that preserve the hue of the image while creating dithered noise (see fig. 7.13). The intensity of this effect can be controlled by the numeric keys 1 through 0. Hold down 1 while executing Hue Protected Noise for the least intensity; hold down 0 for the greatest intensity. Like the Glass Lens filters, the Hue Protected Noise function is provided in three filters:

◆ **HUE PROTECTED NOISE MAX.** This filter creates the maximum amount of noise. The intensity keys control a range of 60 percent to 100 percent noise application.

◆ **HUE PROTECTED NOISE MED.** This filter applies a medium amount of noise, with intensity keys controlling a range between 30 percent and 70 percent noise.

◆ **HUE PROTECTED NOISE MIN.** Much more subtle, this filter works in the 1 percent to 40 percent range providing fine control over noise application. At low intensities, an extremely fine grain is produced, adding texture at a subtle yet powerful level.

FIGURE 7.12

The Grime Layer filter applied to an image at 1, 2, 3, 5, and 10 intensity.

FIGURE 7.13
*The Hue Protected Noise filters
applied to an image and to a test
strip of 50 percent gray.*

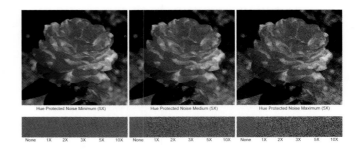

Use Hue Protected Noise filters to add texture to scans or computer-rendered images to give them a more natural, filmlike appearance. Use them on gradient blends to eliminate banding effects, producing a textured gradient. Subtle applications of noise can be particularly useful on textures created for 3D models and 3D rendering, providing a more realistic, dirtied appearance.

Special Red, Green, and Blue Noises

Another set of three Noise filters, the Special Noises, provide separate red, green, and blue noise generation (see fig. 7.14). The intensity of this effect can be controlled through the numeric keys 1 through 0. Hold down 1 while executing Special Noise for

the least intensity; hold down 0 for the greatest intensity.

What makes the Special Noise filters unusual is that the red, green, and blue filters use different color and opacity schemes based on gradients in the Gradient Designer. This results in noise with varying color intensity and transparency. A different noise pattern is created in the red, green, and blue filters.

Use Special Noise on feathered selections or text to fill with a colored sandstone or granite look. Fill a selection with all three to create a variation on a standard RGB noise fill. Try running the Find Edges filters after Special Noise to accentuate the detail.

FIGURE 7.14
*The Special Noise filters applied
to an image and to a test strip
of white color.*

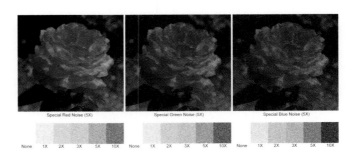

Color Effect Filters

The color group of KPT filters operates on an image or selection's colors, altering the colors in various ways. The color filters include Find Edges, Sharpen Intensity, Fade Contrast, and Color Cyclone (Macintosh only) filters.

Find Edges and Invert

The Find Edges and Invert filter, when applied to an image, outlines and accentuates the contour lines or transitions between colors (see fig. 7.15). The regular Find Edges filter found in Photoshop reverses or "inverts" an image's color, also known as an image's color map, and creates a negative image. The KPT Find Edges and Invert filter performs the Find Edges function, but then inverts the color map again to create a positive image.

The intensity of this effect can be controlled through the numeric keys 1 through 0. Hold down 1 while executing Find Edges and Invert for the least intensity; hold down 0 for the greatest intensity.

If you hold down the Caps Lock key while executing the Find Edges and Invert filter, the invert part of Find Edges and Invert function is toggled off, creating a negative color image.

When applied at high intensity, the Find Edges and Invert filter produces stained glass-like effects, with inordinate amounts of detail depending on the source image. When applied at very low intensity, the filter produces faint outlines against a white background.

Find Edges Charcoal

The Find Edges Charcoal filter provides an alternate, softer version of the Find Edges and Invert filter. In some cases, faint grayish lines give the appearance of a charcoal rendering. The intensity of this effect can be controlled through the numeric keys 1 through 0. Hold down 1 while executing Find Edges Charcoal for the least intensity; hold down 0 for the greatest intensity. If you hold down the Caps Lock key while executing the Find Edges Charcoal filter, the invert function of Find Edges Charcoal function is toggled off, creating a negative color image.

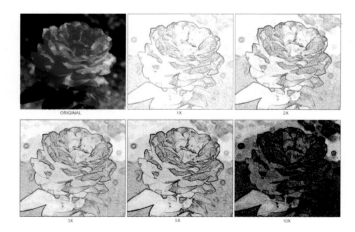

FIGURE 7.15

The Find Edges and Invert filter applied to an image at 1, 2, 3, 5, and 10 intensity.

When used on feathered selections, the Find Edges Charcoal creates a white halo bordering the selection. The effects of the Find Edges Charcoal filter are more subtle than the Find Edges and Invert filter. Try using it on a color image with the Caps Lock key depressed. This creates a soft, iridescent neon look against a black background.

Find Edges Soft

The Find Edges Soft creates an even softer find edges effect than the other two Find Edges filters, generating smooth curved outlines around edges (see fig. 7.18). This algorithm also is different in that it does not invert again to a white background (positive image), but stays as black background (negative image). The intensity of this effect can be controlled through the numeric keys 1 through 0. Hold down 1 while executing Find Edges Soft for the least intensity; hold down 0 for the greatest intensity.

Try repeated applications of Find Edges Soft at intensity 5. Then adjust the image's brightness and contrast levels using Photoshop's Auto-Adjust Levels

function or your image processing application's brightness/contrast controls to brighten or equalize the levels. This can produce some wild, neon-like or glowing translucent tube effects. Or, try the same thing with an intensity of 10 and no Level Adjust function.

If you hold down the Caps Lock key while executing the Find Edges Soft filter, the image or selection's color map is inverted, creating a positive color image (similar to the Find Edges and Invert filter).

Sharpen Intensity

The Sharpen Intensity filter increases the color contrast, brightening up the overall image and making the color appear more vivid (see fig. 7.17). The intensity of this effect can be controlled through the numeric keys 1 through 0. Hold down 1 while executing Sharpen Intensity for the least intensity; hold down 0 for the greatest intensity.

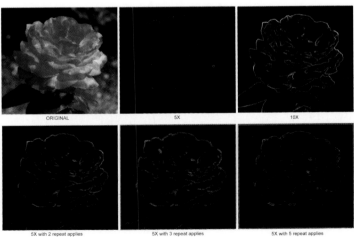

FIGURE 7.16
The Find Edges Soft filter applied to an image at 1, 2, 3, 5, and 10 intensity.

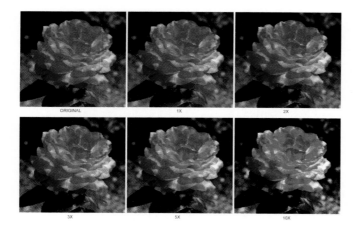

Use the Sharpen Intensity filter on entire images or selected areas to beef up the colors or increase the color saturation. Extreme intensity or repeated applications will have a posterization effect. Light applications provide a subtle color enhancement or remove a dull haze layer from an image. Use Sharpen Intensity to help restore images that suffer saturation loss upon conversion to CMYK color format.

Fade Contrast

The Fade Contrast filter performs the opposite effect of the Sharpen Intensity filter. Fade Contrast provides a graying effect to an image by measuring the average relative contrast between pixels, then fading the contrast of the pixels (see fig. 7.18). The intensity of this effect can be controlled through the numeric keys 1 through 0. Hold down 1 while executing Fade Contrast for the least intensity; hold down 0 for the greatest intensity.

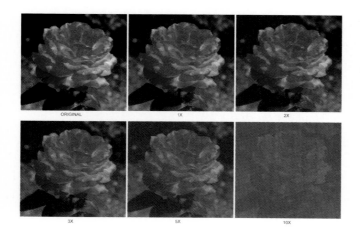

FIGURE 7.18

The Fade Contrast filter applied to an image at 1, 2, 3, 5, and 10 intensity.

The Fade Contrast filter is very useful for highlighting or bringing attention to a specific area of an image. Just select the area, invert the selection, and apply Fade Contrast. This punches out the object of interest by fading the contrast in the surrounding area outside of the object.

Color Cyclone—Macintosh Only

The Color Cyclone filter is more like a tool to generate arbitrary maps. An *arbitrary map* refers to Photoshop's arbitrary maps function, which enables the user to save an image's color table information. An image's color table, also known as a *color curve*, contains information about hue, saturation, and intensity of the pixels in a given image. While altering an image's color curve information is a complex operation, the Color Cyclone filter enables you to alter this information in an iterative visual way (see fig. 7.19). You then can apply the altered color curve to the current image or selection, or save it as an arbitrary map file for later use.

The Color Cyclone filter, when activated by selecting it from Photoshop's Filters/Video menu, begins color cycling the current image's color curve information through endless permutations and variations of colors. While in this mode, several keyboard keys become active and enable you to control various functions of the Color Cyclone filter. These keys are as follows:

◆ →. Speeds up the process of color cycling.

◆ ←. Slows down the process of color cycling.

◆ ↑. Changes the direction of the color cycling.

◆ ↓. Moves to the next arbitrary map.

◆ **?.** Starts Color Cyclone help, a screen showing available keyboard options.

◆ **spacebar.** Pressing and holding the spacebar pauses the color cycling process; release the spacebar to resume.

◆ **0 through 6.** Changes the transition mode or Fade mode between arbitrary maps during color cycling.

◆ **Return (Enter).** Applies the current color cycling state to the underlying image or selection.

◆ **S.** Saves the current state as an arbitrary map file. This file is a custom arbitrary map file containing the hue, color, and intensity curves. You can press the S key any time while viewing the color cycling to save out an arbitrary map file. Each time this occurs, the file saves as the name "Cyclone Arbmap date.n" where date is expressed as YYMMDD and n is the number of the map file created on the aforementioned date. The first arbitrary map file saved on January 2, 1995 would have the filename "Cyclone Arbmap 950102.1"

Once saved, the arbitrary map file can be retrieved and applied to another image. This is done in one of two ways depending on which version of Photoshop you are running. In Photoshop 2.5, the function exists under the Image/Map/Arbitrary menu. In Photoshop 3.0, the function exists under the Image/Map/Curves menu. In each case, the dialog contains a load function to load an arbitrary map file (see fig. 7.20).

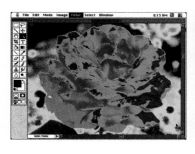

FIGURE 7.19

Color Cyclone in action (left) and captured map file applied to an image (right).

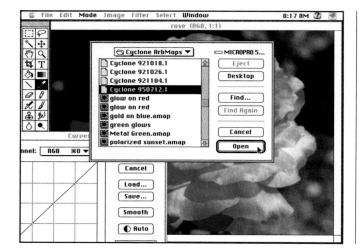

FIGURE 7.20

Loading an arbitrary map file containing color curve information.

Loading the arbitrary map file and clicking on OK will apply the color curve information found in the arbitrary map file to the underlying image or selection. Several already-created arbitrary map files can be found in the KPT Support Files directory in a folder called Cyclone Arbmaps.

Color Cyclone operates on RGB color images, but try using it on a grayscale image converted to RGB for some interesting results.

NOTE *Arbitrary map files created with Color Cyclone under Macintosh Photoshop 3.0 are completely compatible with Windows Photoshop 3.0 with no conversion necessary! Just copy the file from the Mac onto a DOS disk, rename it to the DOS eight-character file name with a .AMP extension. Several arbitrary map files are included on the accompanying CD-ROM disk in the ARBMAPS directory. You can load them in Windows Photoshop choosing Image/Adjust/Curves and then selecting Load. Select the .AMP file from the CD-ROM and you will see its color curve applied to the underlying image or selection.* ●

Blur Filters

The blur group of filters utilize custom Gaussian-style or Motion Blur filters to produce a wide variety of blurring effects to an image or selection. The Blur filters include the Smudge and Gaussian Blur filters.

The Smudge Left/Smudge Right Lighten and Darken Filters

The Smudge filters are symmetrical, directional, multi-level Motion Blur filters that utilize a Lighten or Darken Apply mode (see fig. 7.21). These filters are unique in that the effects are constrained to a horizontal axis. Think of these filters as oil paintbrushes, enabling you to smudge and smear the details of your image left and right, making them lighter or darker in the process. The intensity of this effect can be controlled through the numeric keys 1 through 0. Hold down 1 while executing the Smudge Filters for the least intensity; hold down 0 for the greatest intensity.

Try combining the lighten and darken filters for interesting blends. Because the filter uses a multi-layer blurry blend, the Smudge Left Darken and Smudge

Right Lighten do not cancel each other out, but instead create an interesting blended blur effect. Repeated applications of one Smudge filter blurs the pixels into thin needle-like shapes. Utilizing one direction of Smudge filters can create motion trails behind or leading an object or selection.

Gaussian Electrify—Macintosh Only

Gaussian Electrify, like the Gaussian Glow filter, combines processes that previously took several steps into a one step operation. The Gaussian Electrify filter creates a soft, light glowing effect on an image or selection while retaining the fine detail (see fig. 7.22). The effect is similar to the old photographer's trick of smearing a small amount of Vaseline on a camera lens to create a soft focus effect. Gaussian Electrify works best on images with a well-lit subject against a dark background, creating a beautiful soft aura around the subject.

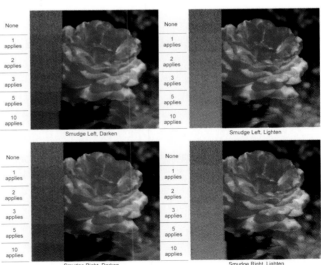

FIGURE 7.21

The Smudge Filters applied to an image and to a section of gray noise.

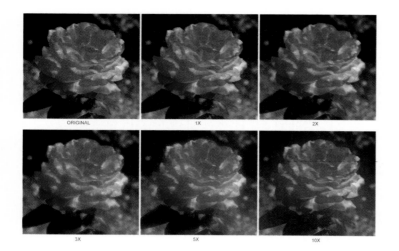

FIGURE 7.22

The Gaussian Electrify filter applied to an image at 1, 2, 3, 5, and 10 intensity.

The intensity of the Gaussian Electrify effect can be controlled through the numeric keys 1 through 0. Hold down 1 while executing Gaussian Electrify for the least intensity; hold down 0 for the greatest intensity. Higher intensities will result in a lighter image.

Gaussian Glow—Macintosh Only

The Gaussian Glow filter works in a manner similar to the Gaussian Electrify filter, but has a darkening effect that intensifies the color while retaining the fine detail. This effect gives the appearance of bleeding or running colors, like an old photograph (see fig. 7.23).

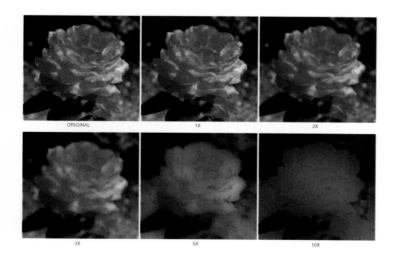

FIGURE 7.23

The Gaussian Glow filter applied to an image at 1, 2, 3, 5, and 10 intensity.

The intensity of the Gaussian Glow effect can be controlled through the numeric keys 1 through 0. Hold down 1 while executing Gaussian Glow for the least intensity; hold down 0 for the greatest intensity. Higher intensities will result in a darker image.

Gaussian Weave—Macintosh Only

The Gaussian Weave filter uses two directional Gaussian Blur effects with a lighten apply mode to create a weave-like blurring pattern on an image or selection. Repeated applications of the Gaussian Weave filter on an image will create interesting color weaves (see fig. 7.24).

The intensity of the Gaussian Weave effect can be controlled through the numeric keys 1 through 0. Hold down 1 while executing Gaussian Glow for the least intensity; hold down 0 for the greatest intensity. Higher intensities will result in a more distorted image.

FIGURE 7.24

The Gaussian Weave filter applied to an image at 1, 2, 3, 5, and 10 intensity.

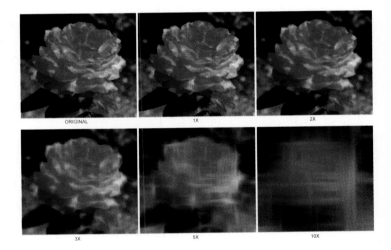

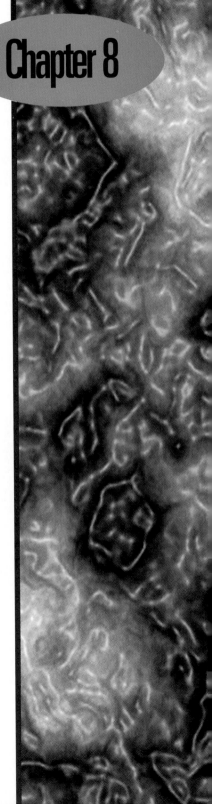

Chapter 8

Other Filters and Utilities

$\mathscr{I}$n addition to the filters discussed in Chapter 7, KPT includes a few other filters and utilities for specific operations. This chapter provides information on the 3D Stereo Noise and Page Curl filters, along with the Seamless Welder and Selection Info utilities.

3D Stereo Noise

Although technically the 3D Stereo Noise filter falls into the Noise category, its primary purpose is to produce stereogram images (see fig. 8.1). Stereograms simulate 3D pictures comprised of black-and-white dots dispersed in a noise pattern. These pictures, when viewed slightly out of focus, reveal patterns and shapes that take on three-dimensional depth properties. Not everyone is capable of achieving the relaxed focus necessary to view these images, but those who can view them observe shapes that exist at different ranges along the Z (depth) axis.

The process usually begins with a grayscale image. The filter generates a noise pattern along horizontal frequencies that relate to the corresponding levels of gray contained within the image. Black colors correspond to very low frequencies, where whites correspond to high frequencies. The higher a gray level's frequency, the closer it appears in the 3D effect. White figures appear close up, while black figures appear farther away. Levels of gray between black and white appear somewhere in the middle, dependent on how weighted the gray level is toward black or white.

You have the ability to adjust the overall range of depth used in the effect, creating a shallow or deep viewing space. The amount of depth within the effect can be controlled through the use of the keyboard's numeric keys 1 through 9. These number keys serve to increase or decrease the horizontal frequency of the pattern, in turn increasing or decreasing the amount of depth applied to the image. Holding down 1 while executing the 3D Stereo Noise filter on an image creates the effect with very shallow depth properties. Holding down 9 while executing the filter creates an image with extreme depth properties. The default setting is 5.

To create a 3D Stereo Noise image or stereogram, start with an image filled with a medium gray. Add some

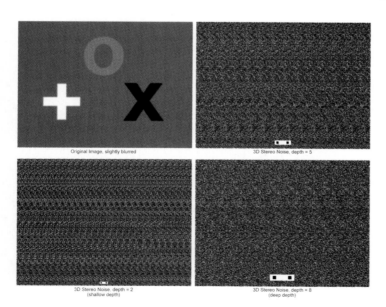

Original Image, slightly blurred

3D Stereo Noise, depth = 5

3D Stereo Noise, depth = 2
(shallow depth)

3D Stereo Noise, depth = 8
(deep depth)

FIGURE 8.1

3D Stereo Noise.

simple shapes or text consisting of solid grayscale colors like black, white, and non-medium gray. Then, process them with a slight blur filter to soften the edges. Blurring the edges makes the shapes easier to see once the 3D Stereo Noise filter has processed them. Now run the 3D Stereo Noise filter, found under your plug-in compatible application's Filters menu, with a depth setting of 5.

By default, the filter will create a small white box containing two black squares at the bottom of the image. These squares are meant as an aid to converging your eyes on the 3D Stereo image. By shifting your focus to a deeper point within the image, the small black squares will start converging together. When the squares merge into one, you have achieved the proper focus point for viewing

the image. These squares can be omitted by holding down the Caps Lock while executing the 3D Stereo Noise filter.

The Page Curl Filter

The Page Curl filter, found under your plug-in compatible application's Filters menu, creates the effect of a page corner being turned over (see fig. 8.2). The filter automatically adds a specular highlight and shadow for the curl and makes the curl slightly translucent if needed. The filter begins in one corner of an image or selection, and curls on a diagonal to the opposite corner. The origin of the curl is controlled by the keyboard's numeric keys (see table 8.1), which enable you to choose from which corner of the image or selection the effect starts.

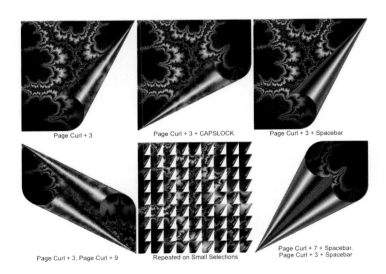

Page Curl + 3

Page Curl + 3 + CAPSLOCK

Page Curl + 3 + Spacebar

Page Curl + 3, Page Curl + 9

Repeated on Small Selections

Page Curl + 7 + Spacebar,
Page Curl + 3 + Spacebar

FIGURE 8.2

The Page Curl filter.

TABLE 8.1

Curl Origin Keys

Key	Effect
7	Starts curl in upper left corner
9	Starts curl in upper right corner
1	Starts curl in lower left corner
3	Starts curl in lower right corner

The orientation of the Page Curl filter is controlled by the state of the Caps Lock key (see table 8.2).

NOTE *To make the page curl effect completely opaque (containing no translucency) hold down the space bar while executing the Page Curl filter.* •

Although the classic page curl effect has become somewhat of a graphics cliché, try using the Page Curl filter for other unique effects. When used on multiple thin rectangular selections, a louvre-like pattern can be created. Used on small or irregular adjacent selections, a frayed edge or hairlike effect can be obtained.

TABLE 8.2

Page Curl Orientation Controls

Key	Effect
Caps On	Creates curl with vertical orientation
Caps Off	Creates curl with horizontal orientation

The Seamless Welder

The Texture Explorer extension generates textures that are seamless, meaning there are no apparent seams when the texture is tiled adjacently into a selection or image. If you want to take another texture that does not have seamless properties and make it seamless, the Seamless Welder utility is an option. The Seamless Welder, found under your plug-in compatible application's Filters menu, takes a rectangular selection and processes the pixels to give the impression of a seamless tiling texture. For the utility to work properly, you must have an image open that contains a rectangular selection area within (see fig. 8.3).

The selection must be contained within a larger area because the utility reads information from the pixels surrounding the selection to create the seamless effect. If you attempt to run Seamless Welder on a selection with little or no bordering pixels, you'll receive an error message stating that you must leave at least 10 percent of the overall image outside the selection area.

The intensity of the Seamless Welder inside the selection area is controlled by the keyboard's numeric keys 1 through 9. Hold down the 9 key while executing the Seamless Welder for the maximum welding effect, producing a perfect seamless tiling region. Hold down the 1 key for a subtle, less noticeable welding effect.

When a rectangular selection has been processed with the Seamless Welder facility, try using it as a tileable texture within a larger image. In Photoshop, you can use the Edit/Define Pattern command to define the selection as a tileable pattern, then use Edit/Fill/Pattern to fill it into a larger area.

A traditional method of creating seamless tiles involves using an offset filter to take a selection's edges and shift them into the center of the image. Then,

FIGURE 8.3

Seamless Welder filter.

Making a Rectangular Selection

Seamless Welder Applied

The Welded Selection Filled into a Larger Image

using a cloning or rubber stamp tool, you can remove the seams by painting in soft copies of the surrounding area over the seams. This method works well unless there is severely sharp color transitions between the seams. The Seamless Welder utility can bridge the gap between this traditional method and using the Texture Explorer's algorithmically perfect textures. Try using it on complex images like sections of photos or other images. Remember to leave yourself enough room outside of the selection so that the Seamless Tile can create a good weld.

Selection Info

The Selection Info utility is a useful tool for providing dimensional information about a given selection within an image (see fig. 8.4). The main purpose of this utility is to help you calculate the percentage of the overall image that is used by the selection area, as well as to calculate the physical size in bytes of the selection. This can be helpful for interface designers who require maximum control over utilization of all available screen area when designing an interface screen.

You can access the Selection Info utility from your plug-in compatible application's Filters menu, under the KPT 2.0 Extensions menu. For this utility to work, a rectangular selection must exist within the given image, or the entire image will be used for the calculations.

Selection Info yields the following information:

◆ The dimensions (in pixels) of the rectangular area

◆ The number of pixels within the area

◆ The percentage of the overall image utilized in the selection

The physical size of the selection in bytes can be calculated by multiplying the total bytes contained in the entire image (typically the file size in bytes) by the percentage used in the selection, yielding the total bytes used in the selection.

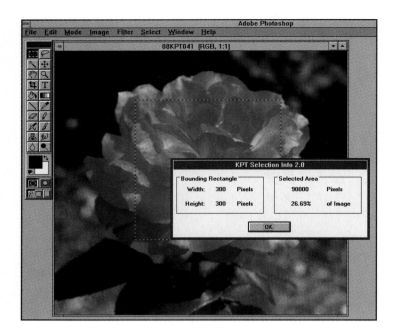

FIGURE **8.4**

Selection Info 2.0 dialog box.

Part *IV*

Using KPT

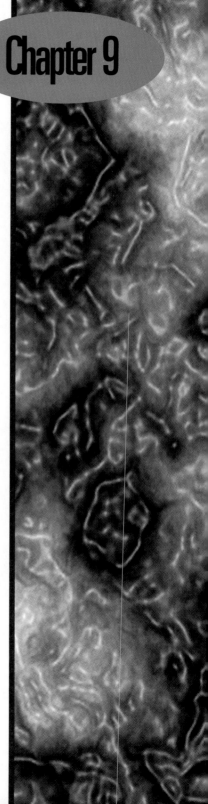

Chapter 9

Putting It All Together

𝒯here are countless ways to use KPT in the creation of your artwork. In the following chapter, you will examine a sampling of the ways the KPT suite of tools can be used to create different types of art, from color to black and white. These examples utilize both the KPT extensions and the KPT filters to achieve their goals.

Creating a Spot Ad with KPT

KPT can be used as the "glue" that combines scanned and 3D-rendered imagery into a composite image. Start by acquiring a scan or image of some clouds for use as a foundation layer.

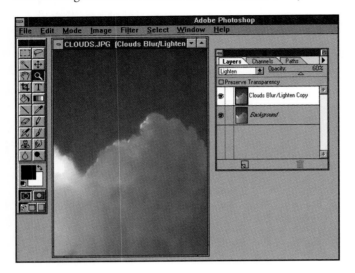

FIGURE 9.1

Copy the cloud background layer to a new layer (Layer 2). Apply a Gaussian Blur filter to Layer 2. Then change Layer 2's apply mode to Lighten at 70 percent opacity.

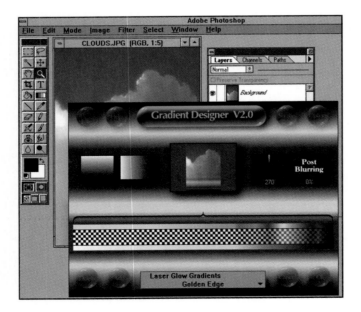

FIGURE 9.2

Merge Layer 2 and the background layer into one. (Macintosh users can forgo the previous steps and just apply the KPT Gaussian Glow filter to the cloud scan). Now start the KPT Gradient Designer and load the preset Laser/Golden Edge. Compress the gradient to the right, by using Option+click (Mac) or Alt+click (Windows) and dragging in the gradient bar. Then apply the gradient to the image by clicking on OK.

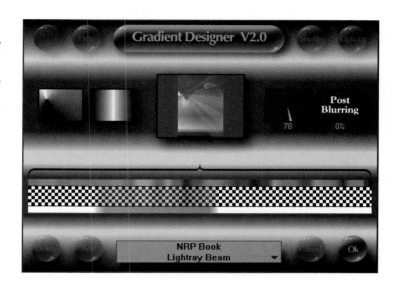

FIGURE 9.3

Restart the Gradient Designer and load the preset NRP Book/Lightray Beam. *Position the direction control to taste, then apply the gradient to the image by clicking on OK.*

FIGURE 9.4

Add a plane. In this case a 32-bit, 3D-rendered image was composited onto the clouds using the image's 8-bit Alpha Channel as the transparency information.

FIGURE 9.5

Add a lens flare effect to emulate the sun, and set intensity at 120 percent.

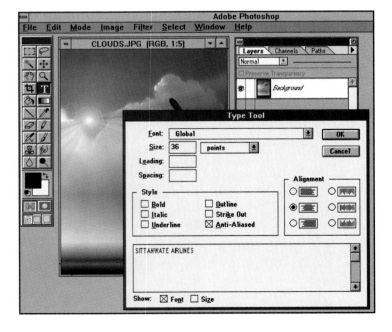

FIGURE 9.6

Add basic type to the image.

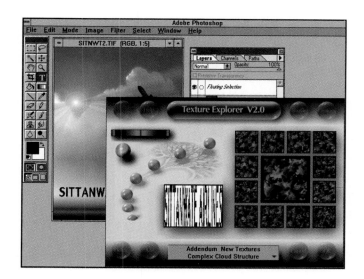

FIGURE 9.7

Start the Texture Explorer, and find a suitable texture. In this case a dark translucent effect was desired. Use the Procedural Blend Apply mode to blend the texture into the type.

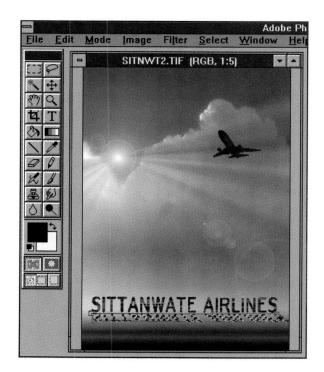

FIGURE 9.8

With the type selected, copy and flip to create a shadow. Distort the shadow selection to create the illusion of a light source.

FIGURE 9.9

Adjust the shadow selection's opacity, then drop onto the image.

FIGURE 9.10

The final composite image, slightly cropped at the bottom to enhance to ground effect.

Creating Translucent 3D Light Rays

The Gradient Designer can be used to generate some really beautiful light ray effects. Start by opening a new RGB image. Then, apply the KPT Grime Layer filter at the default intensity setting.

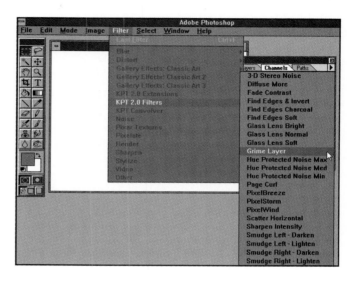

FIGURE 9.11

Applying the Grime Layer filter.

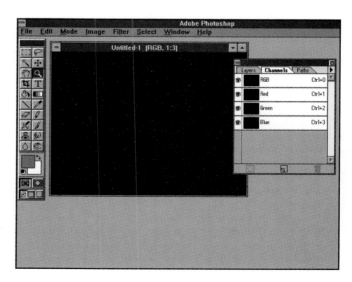

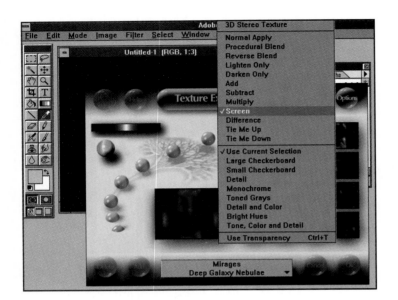

FIGURE 9.13

Start the Texture Explorer and load the preset Mirages/Deep Galaxy Nebulae. *Set the tiling size to Tile Size of Selection and the apply mode to Screen. Then click on OK to apply the texture to the underlying image.*

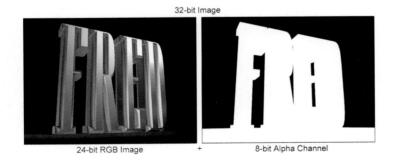

32-bit Image

24-bit RGB Image   +   8-bit Alpha Channel

FIGURE 9.14

Create or import some 3D text. In this case, a 32-bit image created in a 3D rendering program was imported using the image's Alpha Channel as transparency information.

FIGURE 9.15

Composite the 3D text onto the underlying image. Make a copy of the 3D text image's Alpha Channel and import it into your new image as a new Alpha Channel.

FIGURE 9.16

Start the Gradient Designer and create a transparent ray-like gradient, or load the preset NRP Book/ Amazing Rays. *Set the apply mode to Screen, and click on OK.*

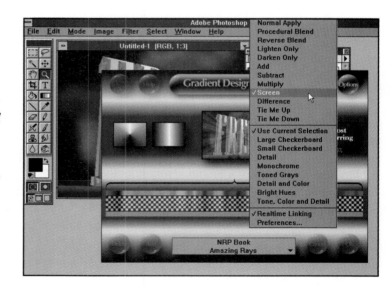

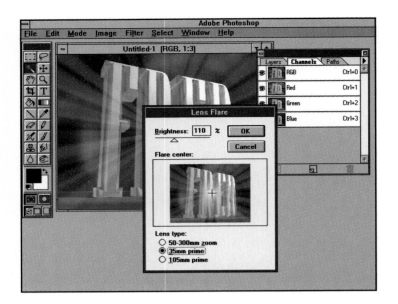

FIGURE 9.17

Apply a lens flare effect at the gradient's origin to create the illusion of a bright sun.

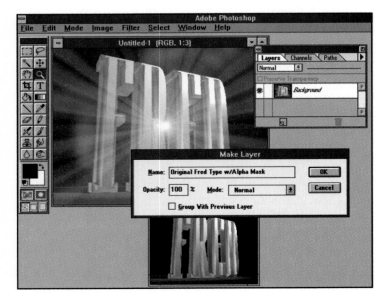

FIGURE 9.18

Create a new image layer (Layer 2) and drop another copy of the 3D text into the layer so that it overlays the original text in Layer 1.

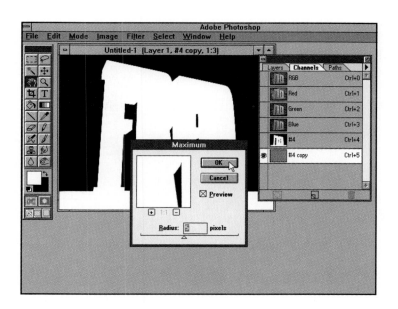

FIGURE 9.19

Now you need to perform some Alpha Channel operations to create a halo effect around the type. In your new image, make a copy of channel 4 (which should contain a copy of the 3D text's Alpha Channel) and call it #4 copy. Apply a Maximum filter to #4 copy.

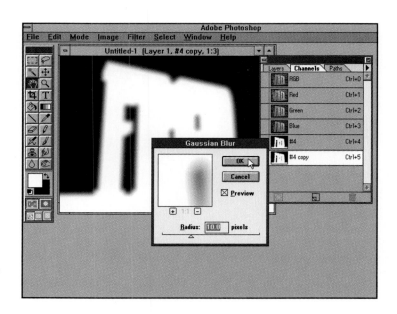

FIGURE 9.20

Apply a Gaussian Blur filter to #4 copy.

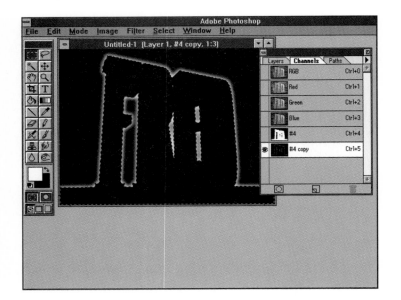

FIGURE 9.21

Load the original Alpha Channel #4 as a selection into #4 copy and fill the selection with black.

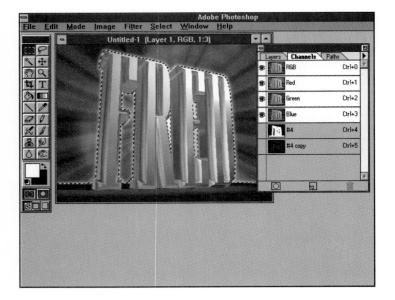

FIGURE 9.22

Load the #4 copy as a selection into the image's RGB Layer 1. Fill the selection with white.

FIGURE 9.23

Use Photoshop's Eraser tool at low opacity (30 percent–50 percent) to erase selected areas of Layer 2 to reveal the light rays in Layer 1. This effect can be duplicated in Fractal Painter by using Painter's cloning tools.

FIGURE 9.24

The final composite image with lens flare effect reapplied at the gradient origin.

Creating Black-and-White Art

KPT is an excellent tool for creating black-and-white art for print. By working in grayscale modes, KPT's color effects are translated to shades of gray with some interesting results. In this case, a scanned image acquired from a rock band was the starting point. The image was then sliced up and rearranged into just the four band member's heads.

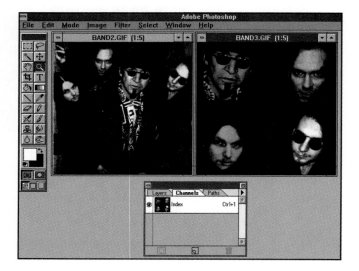

FIGURE 9.25

The scanned image and the newly divided image.

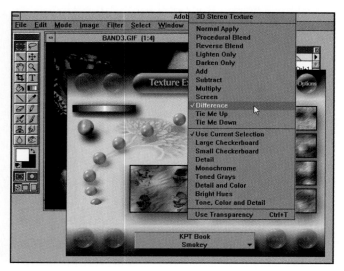

FIGURE 9.26

Start the Texture Explorer and load the preset NRP Book/Smokey. Set the tiling size to Tile Size of Selection, select the Difference Apply mode, and click on OK to apply to the underlying image.

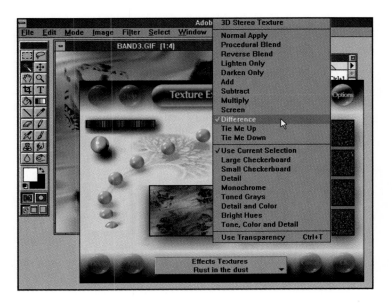

FIGURE 9.27

Restart the Texture Explorer and load the preset Effects Textures/Rust in the Dust. *Set tiling to Tile Size of Selection, select Difference Apply mode, and click on OK.*

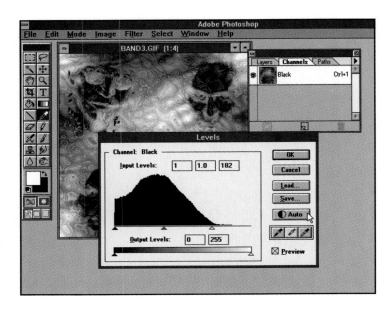

FIGURE 9.28

Use Photoshop's Auto-Levels function or your application's Brightness/Contrast controls to adjust the image's brightness/contrast.

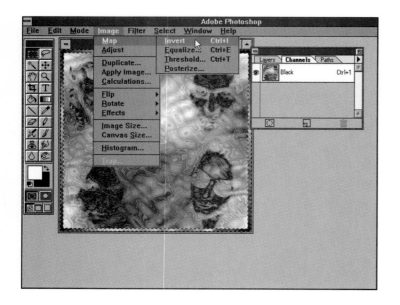

FIGURE 9.29

Create a border around the image by selecting a border area, then inverting the color map.

FIGURE 9.30

The final composite image with glowing type added.

Instant Abstract Art

Use the KPT extensions and filters to quickly create beautiful abstract artwork. Start with a new RGB image. Start the Gradient Designer and load the preset *NRP Book/Color Wheel.* Set the apply mode to Normal and click on OK to apply the gradient to the underlying image.

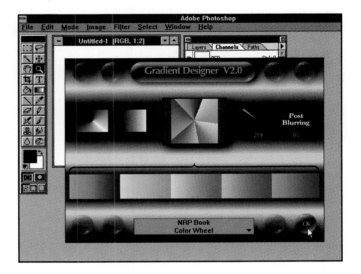

FIGURE 9.31

Start the Gradient Designer and load the preset NRP Book/Color Wheel.

FIGURE 9.32

Start the Texture Explorer and load the preset Effects Textures/Impressionist flowers. *Set tiling to Tile Size of Selection, select Procedural Blend Apply mode, and click on OK.*

FIGURE 9.33

Restart the Texture Explorer and load the preset Eerie/Magenta Ring Nebula. *Set tiling to Tile Size of Selection, select Difference Apply mode, and click on OK.*

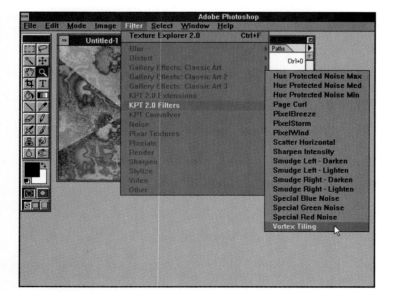

FIGURE 9.34

Apply the KPT Vortex Tiling filter to the image at 6 intensity (depress the 6 key while executing the filter).

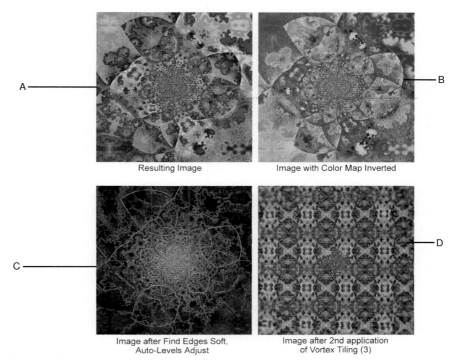

A — Resulting Image

B — Image with Color Map Inverted

C — Image after Find Edges Soft, Auto-Levels Adjust

D — Image after 2nd application of Vortex Tiling (3)

FIGURE 9.35

Observe the result in image A. Take this one step further as shown in the next three images. Image B shows image A with the color map inverted, creating a nice purple/blue color scheme. Image C shows image A after applying KPT's Find Edges Soft filter, then performing Photoshop's Auto-Levels function to adjust the image's brightness/contrast levels. Image D shows image A after re-applying the Vortex Tiling filter at 3 intensity, producing an interesting pattern.

The KPT Gradient Designer for 3D Studio

HSC has released a special version of the Gradient Designer that works with 3D applications like Autodesk's 3D Studio. This special version of the Gradient Designer known as the Gradient Designer IPAS (IPAS is the term for 3D Studio's external plug-ins) enables you to create animated gradients. Animated gradients are gradients that change over time. The KPT Gradient Designer IPAS enables the user to manipulate the gradient's parameters like algorithm, looping, origin, color, and other parameters to change over time. In addition, the KPT Gradient Designer IPAS enables the user to overlay multiple layers of animated gradients into a composite animation. In figure 9.36, observe the Gradient Designer interface running from within 3D Studio's Material's Editor.

FIGURE 9.36

The Gradient Designer interface running from within 3D Studio.

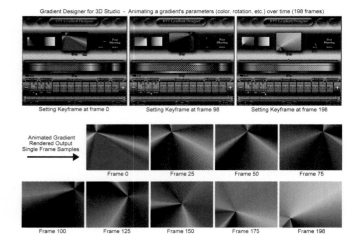

FIGURE 9.37

The top half of this figure illustrates setting a beginning, middle, and end keyframe for an animated gradient sequence. The bottom half of the figure shows actual animated output over time (frames).

FIGURE 9.38

A texture bitmap created with the KPT Texture Explorer is loaded as a still background image for the KPT Gradient Designer IPAS.

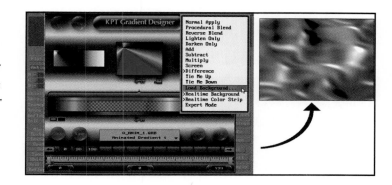

FIGURE 9.39

This figure illustrates the rendered output with the new background inserted, and the gradient's apply mode set to Difference. Once created, this composite animation is saved as a Gradient Designer IPAS preset for later use.

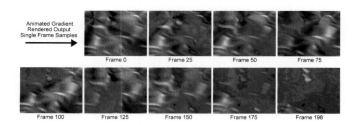

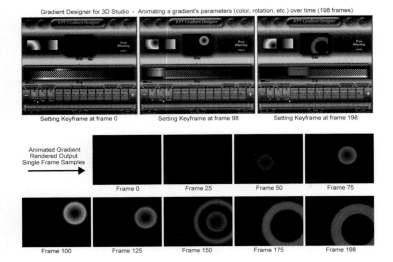

Gradient Designer for 3D Studio - Animating a gradient's parameters (color, rotation, etc.) over time (198 frames)

Setting Keyframe at frame 0 Setting Keyframe at frame 98 Setting Keyframe at frame 198

Animated Gradient
Rendered Output
Single Frame Samples →

Frame 0   Frame 25   Frame 50   Frame 75

Frame 100   Frame 125   Frame 150   Frame 175   Frame 198

FIGURE 9.40

Now you create a second layer of animated gradient. The second layer's animated output is shown in the bottom half of the figure.

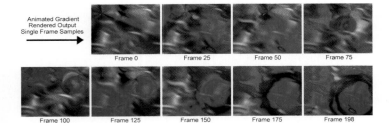

Animated Gradient
Rendered Output
Single Frame Samples →

Frame 0   Frame 25   Frame 50   Frame 75

Frame 100   Frame 125   Frame 150   Frame 175   Frame 198

FIGURE 9.41

Next, the first layer preset created previously is loaded as a background into gradient Layer 2, and Layer 2's apply mode is set to Difference. The composite animated output is illustrated here. The new Layer 2 with the Layer 1 background is saved as a preset for later use.

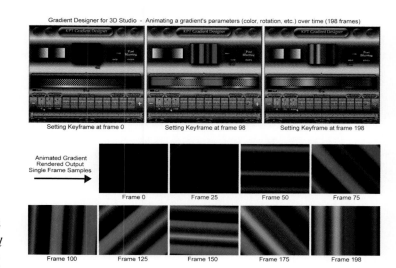

Gradient Designer for 3D Studio - Animating a gradient's parameters (color, rotation, etc.) over time (198 frames)

Setting Keyframe at frame 0   Setting Keyframe at frame 98   Setting Keyframe at frame 198

Animated Gradient
Rendered Output
Single Frame Samples

Frame 0   Frame 25   Frame 50   Frame 75

Frame 100   Frame 125   Frame 150   Frame 175   Frame 198

FIGURE 9.42

Finally, a third layer of animated gradient is created.

FIGURE 9.43

The second layer preset created previously is then loaded as a background in Layer 3, and Layer 3's apply mode is set to Difference. The composite animated output is shown and represents three complete layers of animated gradients interacting with a static background image.

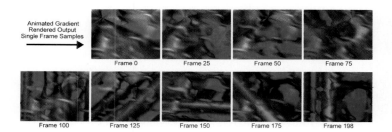

Animated Gradient
Rendered Output
Single Frame Samples

Frame 0   Frame 25   Frame 50   Frame 75

Frame 100   Frame 125   Frame 150   Frame 175   Frame 198

Appendix A

KPT Keystroke Commands

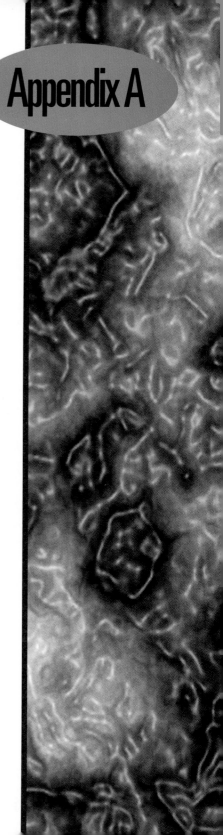

TABLE A.1

Extensions, General

Keystroke	Command
Enter (Return)	Equivalent to clicking on the OK button in the extension.
spacebar	Holding down the space bar while starting a KPT extension displays the extension against a black background. This helps eliminate background clutter, enabling you to focus on the KPT functions.
Escape (Esc) or ⌘+. (Mac)	Equivalent to clicking on the Cancel button in the extension.
A	Add preset.
D	Delete preset.
↑	Previous preset in current category.
↓	Next preset in current category.
Page Up	Previous category, first preset.
Page Down	Next category, first preset.
Home	First category, first preset.
End	Last category, first preset.
?, Shift-/ (Mac) or F1 (Windows)	Equivalent to clicking on the Help button; activates Help screen.
⌘+Z (Mac) or Ctrl+Z (Windows)	Undo
⌘+→ (Mac) or Ctrl+→ (Windows)	Change to next apply mode.
⌘+← (Mac) or Ctrl+← (Windows)	Changes to previous apply mode.
	Windows Users Only
Ctrl	Holding down the Ctrl key while starting a KPT extension bypasses loading the proxy background image. This can save you time when working with large images.
?	Changes the cursor into a cursor/question mark, indicating that you now are in context-sensitive Help mode. Click on any button or window in the extension interface to receive help on that particular function.

TABLE A.2

The Gradient Designer

Keystroke	Command
	Within the Gradient Bar Only
⌘+X (Mac) or Ctrl + X (Windows)	Cuts the current selection (area within the Movable Bracket) to the KPT Clipboard.
⌘+C (Mac) or Ctrl+C (Windows)	Copies the current selection to the KPT Clipboard.
⌘+V (Mac) or Ctrl+V (Windows)	Pastes the contents of the KPT Clipboard into the area within the Movable Bracket.
⌘+F (Mac) or Ctrl+F (Windows)	Flips the gradient area within the Movable Bracket.
⌘+I (Mac) or Ctrl+I (Windows)	Inverts the colors in the current selection.
⌘+click/hold (Mac) or Ctrl+click/hold (Windows)	Rotates the current selection.
Option+click/hold (Mac) or Alt+click/hold (Windows)	Compresses or expands the current selection.
	Color Picking Only
Numbers keys 1-0	Holding down a numeric key while picking a color sets the opacity level for the selection area.
	Movable Bracket Commands (Macintosh Only)
Shift+click/hold	When clicking on the center of the Movable Bracket, this enables you to move the entire bracket left or right by the width of the Movable Bracket. When clicking on the right or left side of the Movable Bracket, this enables you to move the bracket end left or right in even increments.
	Miscellaneous Preferences Commands (Macintosh Only)
⌘+P	Activates user preferences.
Option	Holding down the Option key while starting the Gradient Designer sets the user preferences to Return to Previous State.
Shift	Holding down the Shift key while starting the Gradient Designer sets the user preferences to Load Normal Gradient.

continues

TABLE A.2, CONTINUED

The Gradient Designer

Keystroke	Command
Option+Shift	Holding down the Option and Shift keys while starting the Gradient Designer sets the user preferences to Load Smooth Gradient.
Movable Bracket Commands (Windows Only)	
←	Moves the Movable Bracket left one pixel.
→	Moves the Movable Bracket right one pixel.
Shift+←	Moves the entire Movable Bracket to the left by width of Movable Bracket.
Shift+→	Moves the entire Movable Bracket to the right by width of Movable Bracket.
Miscellaneous Commands (Windows Only)	
R	Holding down the R key dynamically toggles the Realtime Linking feature while the key is depressed.

TABLE A.3

The Texture Explorer

Keystroke	Command
⌘+T (Mac) or Ctrl+T (Windows)	Toggles on and off the Transparency option.
Macintosh Users Only	
Caps Lock	Forces tiling size to Tile Size of Selection without affecting current apply mode.
Windows Users Only	
Ctrl+E	Launches the Equalizer function.
Ctrl+S	Toggles on and off constrained mode (sets the Texture to non-tileable mode).
Ctrl+G	Starts the Gradient Designer. Extension from within the Texture Explorer.

Table A.4

The Fractal Explorer

Keystroke	Command
	Windows Users Only
Ctrl+G	Starts the Gradient Designer Extension from within the Fractal Explorer.

Table A.5

The Filters

Keystroke	Command
	All Filters Except Glass Lens, Page Curl, 3D Stereo Noise, and Color Cyclone
1-0	Holding down the numeric keys 1-0 while executing a KPT filter sets the intensity of the filter application from 1 (lightest) to 0 (heaviest).

Table A.6

Glass Lens

Keystroke	Command
1-9	Holding down the numeric keys 1-9 sets the origin of the light to the corresponding position on the numeric keypad.
0	Holding down 0 creates a backlight effect.
Caps Lock	Enabling Caps Lock fills area around sphere with black.
	Windows Users Only
Scroll Lock	Holding down Scroll Lock creates an eclipse effect.

Table A.7

Page Curl

Keystroke	Command
1, 3, 7, and 9	Holding down these keys sets the origin of the page curl to the lower left, lower right, upper left, and upper right respectively.

continues

TABLE A.7 CONTINUED

Page Curl

Keystroke	Command
Caps Lock	Enabling Caps Lock sets the orientation of the page curl to Vertical; disabling Caps Lock sets the orientation of the page curl to horizontal.

TABLE A.8

3D Stereo Noise

Keystroke	Command
1-9	Holding down 1-9 keys sets the depth of the 3D Stereo Noise effect from 1 (shallowest) to 9 (deepest).

TABLE A.9

Color Cyclone-Macintosh Only

Keystroke	Command
	While Cyclone is Running
→	Speed up color cycling.
←	Slow down color cycling.
↑	Change direction of color cycling.
↓	Chooses next arbitrary map.
?	Displays cyclone help.
S	Saves current state as arbitrary map file.
0-6	Changes the fade mode of the cycling.
Enter (Return)	Applies cyclone to the underlying image.

Gallery of Images

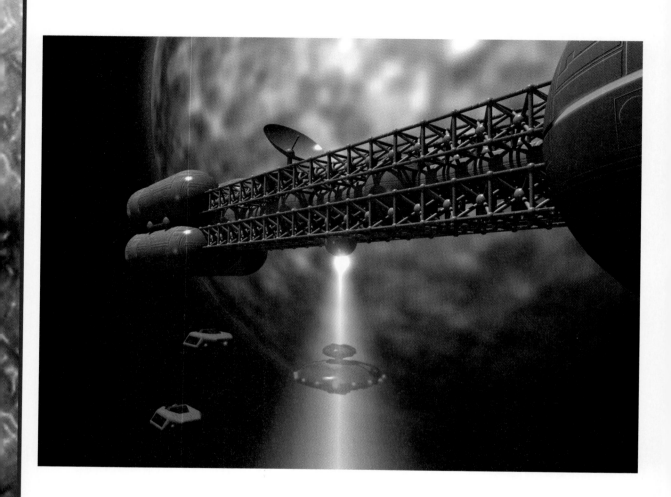

KAI'S POWER TOOLS FILTERS AND EFFECTS

KAI'S POWER TOOLS FILTERS AND EFFECTS

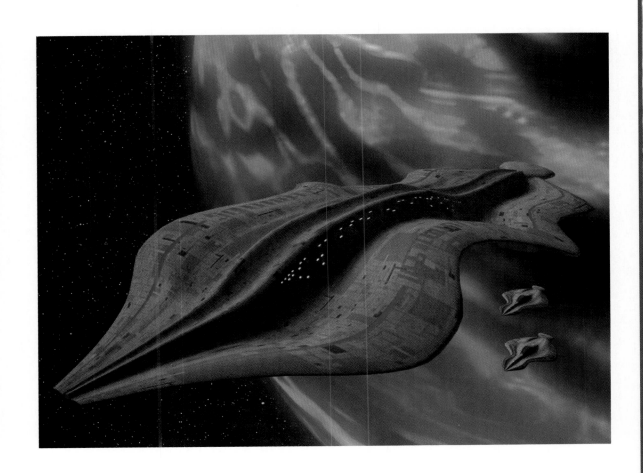

KAI'S POWER TOOLS FILTERS AND EFFECTS

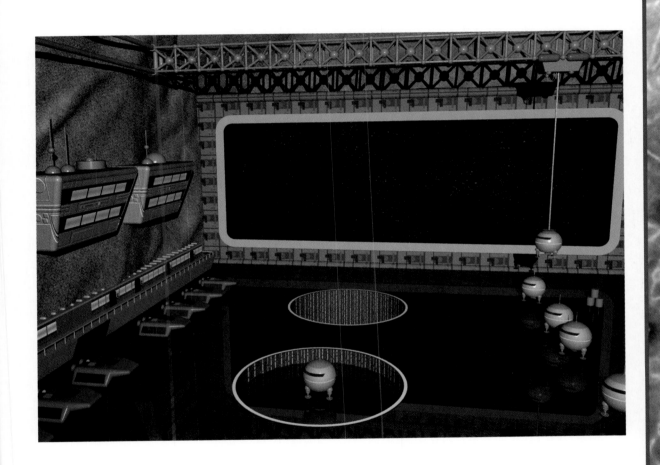

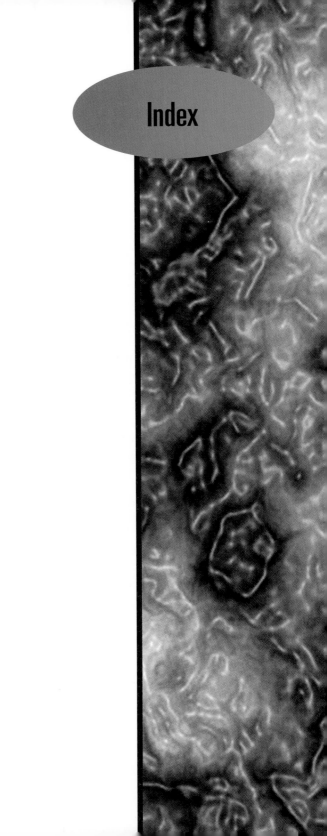

Index

Symbols

A

B

E

F

L

launching
    extensions, 14
    filters, 14
    Gradient Designer, 42
light rays (Gradient Designer), 179
Lighten Apply mode, 30
Linear Blend (Gradient Designer), 46
linking Realtime Preview window
    (Gradient Designer), 51
Logo button, 23
Looping Control menu
    Designer Gradient, 48-49
    Gradient Designer, 48-49
    Gradients on Paths, 86

M

Macintosh
    filters, 11
        Color Cyclone, 159-163
        Gaussian Electrify, 161-162
        Gaussian Glow, 162-163
        Gaussian Weave, 163
    floating point coprocessors, 9
    hardware requirements, 8-9
    installation, 10-11
    keyboard, 12
    software, 10
    troubleshooting INITs, 17
    Windows version, 11-12
Mandelbrot, Benoit (fractals), 121
Mandelbrot set (fractals), 128
math coprocessors, 9
memory
    RAM, 9

Windows (troubleshooting), 17
menus
    Looping Control menu
        Designer Gradient, 48-49
        Gradient Designer, 48-49
        Gradients on Paths, 86
    Options menu (Texture Explorer)
        3D Stereo Noise Apply, 103-104
        Global Transparency, 105-117
        Use Transparency, 105
MicroFrontier Color It!, 10
Micrografx PicturePublisher, 10
minimizing interfaces, 23
modes (Equalizer), 108-109
Movable Bracket (Gradient Designer), 52-55
Multiply Apply mode, 32
mutating (Texture Explorer), 97
    Color Mutation Ball, 102
    Texture Mutation Tree, 100-102

N

Noise Apply Mode (Gradients on Paths), 84-86
Noise filters, 153
    3D Stereo Noise filter, 166-167
    Grime Layer, 154
    Hue Protected, 154-155
    Special, 155
Normal Apply, 26
Numerical Input option (Fractal Explorer),
    128-130

O

OK button (quitting), 39
one-step filters, 145
opacity
    Fractal Explorer, 133-135
    Pop-up Color Picker, 62-64

X-Y-Z

PLUG YOURSELF INTO...

THE MACMILLAN INFORMATION SUPERLIBRARY™

Free information and vast computer resources from the world's leading computer book publisher—online!

FIND THE BOOKS THAT ARE RIGHT FOR YOU!

A complete online catalog, plus sample chapters and tables of contents give you an in-depth look at *all* of our books, including hard-to-find titles. It's the best way to find the books you need!

- **STAY INFORMED** with the latest computer industry news through our online newsletter, press releases, and customized Information SuperLibrary Reports.

- **GET FAST ANSWERS** to your questions about MCP books and software.

- **VISIT** our online bookstore for the latest information and editions!

- **COMMUNICATE** with our expert authors through e-mail and conferences.

- **DOWNLOAD SOFTWARE** from the immense MCP library:
  - Source code and files from MCP books
  - The best shareware, freeware, and demos

- **DISCOVER HOT SPOTS** on other parts of the Internet.

- **WIN BOOKS** in ongoing contests and giveaways!

TO PLUG INTO MCP: ➔   **WORLD WIDE WEB: http://www.mcp.com**

GOPHER: gopher.mcp.com

FTP: ftp.mcp.com

WANT MORE INFORMATION?

CHECK OUT THESE RELATED TOPICS OR SEE YOUR LOCAL BOOKSTORE

CAD and 3D Studio

As the number one CAD publisher in the world, and as a Registered Publisher of Autodesk, New Riders Publishing provides unequaled content on this complex topic. Industry-leading products include AutoCAD and 3D Studio. Leading books in this category include *Inside 3D Studio Release 4* and *3D Studio IPAS Filters and Effects*.

Networking

As the leading Novell NetWare publisher, New Riders Publishing delivers cutting-edge products for network professionals. We publish books for all levels of users, from those wanting to gain NetWare Certification, to those administering or installing a network. Leading books in this category include *Inside NetWare 4.1*, *CNE Training Guide: Managing NetWare Systems, Inside TCP/IP, NetWare: The Professional Reference,* and *CNE Short Course.*

Graphics

New Riders provides readers with the most comprehensive product tutorials and references available for the graphics market. Best-sellers include *Inside CorelDRAW! 5, Inside Photoshop 3,* and *Adobe Photoshop 3 Filters and Effects.*

Internet and Communications

As one of the fastest growing publishers in the communications market, New Riders provides unparalleled information and detail on this ever-changing topic area. We publish international best-sellers such as *New Riders' Official Internet Yellow Pages, 2nd Edition,* a directory of over 10,000 listings of Internet sites and resources from around the world, *Riding the Internet Highway, Deluxe Edition, Internet Firewalls and Network Security,* and *Building a Unix Internet Server.*

Operating Systems

Expanding off our expertise in technical markets, and driven by the needs of the computing and business professional, New Riders offers comprehensive references for experienced and advanced users of today's most popular operating systems, including *Understanding Windows 95, Inside Unix, Inside Windows 95, Inside OS/2 Warp Version 3,* and *Inside MS-DOS 6.22.*

Other Markets

Professionals looking to increase productivity and maximize the potential of their software and hardware should spend time discovering our line of products for Word, Excel, and Lotus 1-2-3. These titles include *Inside Word 6 for Windows, Inside Excel 5 for Windows, Inside 1-2-3 Release 5,* and *Inside WordPerfect for Windows.*

Orders/Customer Service **1-800-653-6156**   Source Code **NRP95**

New Riders Publishing   201 West 103rd Street ◆ Indianapolis, Indiana 46290 USA

REGISTRATION CARD

Kai's Power Tools Filters and Effects

Name _____ Title _____

Company _____ Type of business _____

Address _____

City/State/ZIP _____

Have you used these types of books before? ☐ yes ☐ no

If yes, which ones? _____

_____

How many computer books do you purchase each year? ☐ 1–5 ☐ 6 or more

How did you learn about this book? _____

Where did you purchase this book? _____

Which applications do you currently use? _____

_____

Which computer magazines do you subscribe to? _____

_____

What trade shows do you attend? _____

_____

Comments: _____

_____

_____

Would you like to be placed on our preferred mailing list? ☐ yes ☐ no

☐ **I would like to see my name in print!** You may use my name and quote me in future New Riders products and promotions. My daytime phone number is: _____

New Riders Publishing   201 West 103rd Street ◆ Indianapolis, Indiana 46290 USA

Fax to **317-581-4670**   Orders/Customer Service **1-800-653-6156**   Source Code **NRP95**

Fold Here

BUSINESS REPLY MAIL

FIRST-CLASS MAIL PERMIT NO. 9918 INDIANAPOLIS IN

POSTAGE WILL BE PAID BY THE ADDRESSEE

**NEW RIDERS PUBLISHING
201 W 103RD ST
INDIANAPOLIS IN 46290-9058**